FIFTY YEARS OF RESIDENT OUTDOOR EDUCATION
1930-1980
Its Impact on American Education

FIFTY YEARS OF RESIDENT OUTDOOR EDUCATION
1930-1980
Its Impact on American Education

Edited by
William M. Hammerman
San Francisco State University

American Camping Association
Martinsville, Indiana

Library of Congress Cataloging in Publication Data

Fifty Years of Resident Outdoor Education 1930-1980

    1. Outdoor education—History.   I. Hammerman,
William M.
LB1047.F53   371.3'8   80-13523
ISBN 0-87603-055-X

Published 1980 by the American Camping Association
Martinsville, Indiana 46151
Printed in the United States of America

To the thousands of outdoor educators who have contributed, over the past fifty years, to the growth and development of resident outdoor education in America.

CONTENTS

In the pages that follow, the fifty years of innovative programming in what has come to be called *resident outdoor education* are traced; and the evolution from the early beginnings to the present are explored, examined, and explained. The authors, representing rich and diverse backgrounds, have been intimately involved in the development of outdoor education through the operation of programs themselves and the teaching of other leaders. Although three of the moving spirits—Lloyd B. Sharp, Julian Smith, and William G. Vinal—are no longer living, their legacy of dedication and their philosophy are increasingly affecting the education of youth.

Growth in outdoor education has accompanied the awakening of America to the plight of its threatened environment. There is an increased awareness of the problems of overpopulation, pollution through human and chemical wastes, dangerous insecticides and herbicides, protection of endangered species, preservation of wilderness and other natural areas, and provision of more recreation lands for the hordes of people who want to enjoy the natural environment. These concerns, and the recognition that most children today have no firsthand contact with the land in such experiences as growing food and fiber, have brought demands that educators give more attention to the outdoors. Schools are reminded that they must prepare our youth to

handle, as informed and intelligent citizens, the environmental problems that lie ahead if they are to care for, use, and enjoy our battered planet.

Outdoor education has both influenced and been influenced by the increased concern for the environment. The terms *ecology* and *environmental education* have emerged into prominence, to some extent replacing the terms *conservation, balance in nature,* and *interrelationship*. But, whatever the terminology, resident outdoor education throughout its history has placed importance on ecological education. Today's society recognizes more keenly than ever before the need for these programs in outdoor residence centers.

The outdoors was the principal educational vehicle of ancient peoples, and almost the only educational setting of primitive tribes. Its use was advocated by early educational psychologists such as Pestalozzi. In the United States the nature study movement and the school garden movement promoted learning through direct experiences in the outdoors. The organized camping movement, which began in the 1860s, has long advocated the outdoors as a learning climate. Resident outdoor centers as integral parts of school programs are, however, relatively new. From small beginnings they have now increased from coast to coast; and there is considerable evidence that they have influenced the development of attitudes, knowledge, and skills related to understanding, appreciation, and use of the environment.

The authors of this book analyze the impact that resident outdoor education has had on educational philosophy and practice, and they bring together numerous experiences in developing programs. Two aspects of outdoor education are prominent. The first and this is the central theme that runs throughout the book—is that there is need for direct contact with the environment; that some learning makes a deeper impact and is retained longer when a concept or an object is discovered, observed, sensed, and interpreted in the natural setting. This conviction lies behind the rapid growth of programs in the outdoors.

The second aspect relates to living with our fellow creatures. Teachers and students in outdoor resident centers participate in small informal groups on a twenty-four-hour-a-day basis; sharing food, shelter, work, and leisure in a cooperative milieu with concern for one another's needs. Students from many a classroom have returned from such experiences with a stronger sense of purpose, firmer loyalties, greater respect for one another, and improved relationships with their teacher. For many aspects of learning, the resident outdoor education center may well be as close to an ideal situation as is possible for schools to create.

The authors, and especially William Hammerman as editor, are to be commended for making possible through this one volume a greater understanding of the outdoor education movement and of the need for extending its benefits throughout our school systems.

—Reynold E. Carlson

Bloomington, Indiana
January 1980

PREFACE

During the past fifty years, there has appeared on the American educational scene a curricular development that has been known historically by a variety of terms, such as: *camping education, school camping,* and *resident outdoor education.* This instructional innovation has gradually been implemented in an increasing number of schools that utilize the out-of-doors as a *learning laboratory.*

The exact birthdate for resident outdoor education is difficult to pinpoint. Many educators recognize the year 1930 as the beginning of the modern concept of resident outdoor education for the following reasons:

— Hedley S. Dimock and Charles E. Hendry predicted in 1929 that schools would begin to recognize the educational values of camping. They stated, "The next decade will doubtless see schools extending their program through the summer to include the camping experience. Educators will increasingly become aware of the place of the camp in a complete year-long scheme of education."
— Dr. L. B. Sharp's dissertation, "Education and the Summer Camp," was published by Columbia University Press in 1930.
— 1930 was the year that Bernard Mason completed his doctoral dissertation, "Camping and Education," at The Ohio State University.
— Central Washington College of Education initiated a short-term camping program for fifth to eighth grade children in 1930.
— Dr. Donald R. Hammerman identified 1930-1939 as

the "Period of Inception" for camping education in his dissertation, "An Historical Analysis of the Socio-Cultural Factors that Influenced the Development of Camping Education, 1930-1960."

This volume commemorates the fiftieth anniversary of this unique educational program in the United States. The various outdoor educators who have made written contributions to this book have not only been influenced by the outdoor education movement themselves; but they, in turn, have had an impact upon the growth and development of this field. Each individual has been invited to share his perspective of the impact of resident outdoor education upon American education over the past fifty years because of his involvement in outdoor programs.

Although each contributor could be honored for his service and contributions to outdoor education, three individuals who have devoted a lifetime to teaching others about it are commemorated in this publication for having made an impact upon the growth and development of resident outdoor education in America. Hopefully, someone who reads this collection of thoughts and perceptions of the first fifty years of resident outdoor education will compile a similar volume in 2030 A.D. to commemorate outdoor education's centennial year.

—William M. Hammerman
San Francisco, California
January 1980

ACKNOWLEDGEMENTS

The publication of a commemorative book is due to the contributions of many people. The editor wishes to recognize the efforts of those who have made this book a reality.

Thanks to the individual chapter authors who volunteered to organize their thoughts on specific themes or topics as a "labor of love." Their chapters capture the "flavor" of this particular aspect of the American educational scene.

Thanks to the donors of photographs for digging through their files. When appropriate, a credit line has been used with the pictures selected. Special appreciation to the Burgess Publishing Company, Minneapolis, Minnesota, for permission to use photographs from *Teaching in the Outdoors*; to Regional Services of Northern Illinois University, DeKalb, Illinois; to Donald Rettew, professional photographer, who worked with L. B. Sharp in National Camp from 1951-1961, and to Phiz Mezey, photographer for the Sausalito Teacher Education Project, California. The cover photograph was contributed by Norman Skliar, administrator, Outdoor Environmental Education, Nassau BOCES—Salisbury Center, Westbury, New York.

The collection of data summarized in the chapter, "Impact on the Nation's Schools," was due to the assistance of consultants and coordinators in the various state department of education. In some states, professional associations assumed the leadership and circulated the survey-questionnaires. Thanks to the Michigan Association for Health, Physical Education, and Recreation; the New York State Outdoor Education Association; and the Lane Educational Service District, Eugene, Oregon. Thanks, also, to the hundreds of principals, outdoor school coordinators, and camp directors who actually completed the questionnaires. Two graduate students in ECO Education at San Francisco State University, Therese Jeno and Jane Stanfield assisted with the tabulation of data.

A special thanks to Glenn Job, Director of Communications, and his staff at the American Camping Association for their editing, proof-reading, make-up, and production efforts. Thanks to those individuals or groups who, unintentionally, may have been overlooked; you are with the "spirit" of this book.

INFLUENCE OF THE PRE-1930 PERIOD

The 1930 birthdate for the current concept of resident outdoor education was selected for the reasons stated in the preface. As in any movement, there are usually earlier events and activities that contributed to or helped to nurture the genesis of that development. This is particularly true of resident outdoor education in the United States. The "roots" of this innovative curricular development have been well documented through research studies and current literature. This prologue to the fifty-year period, 1930-1980, draws heavily from several studies that reviewed various factors which have influenced the growth and development of outdoor education. (The identification of these studies and sources of quotations are indicated by reference numbers.)

Philosophical Roots

Although it might be stated, historically speaking, that school camping began with the camp established by Frederick William Gunn in 1861 at Washington, Connecticut; its philosophical roots began much earlier than that. Several researchers state that the elements of a philosophical basis for outdoor education can be found in the doctrines of Comenius, Rousseau, and Pestalozzi.

John Amos Comenius (1592-1670) was a strong advocate of sensory learning who believed that the child should experience the actual object of study before reading about it. He thought that the use of the senses—seeing, hearing, tasting, and touching—were the avenues through which children were to come in contact with the natural world. In preparation for the later study of natural sciences, children should first gain acquaintance with objects such as water, earth, fire, rain, plants, and rocks.(9)

Jean-Jacques Rousseau (1712-1778) carried out the ideas of Comenius by educating the boy, Emile, according to principles found in nature. He believed that physical activity was very important in the education of a child. They are curious, he claimed, and this curiosity should be utilized to the fullest. Rosseau preached that education should be more sensory and rational; less literary and linguistic. Rather than learning indirectly from books, children should learn through direct experience.(7) He proclaimed, "Our first teachers are our feet, our hands and our eyes. To substitute books for all these . . . is but to teach us to use the reason of others."(10)

Johann Henrich Pestalozzi (1746-1827) emphasized the use of direct, firsthand experiences and real objects, also. In addition to "reading, writing, and arithmetic," he taught practical skills such as farming, housekeeping, spinning and weaving. The school yard was used for lessons in nature study and geography. His methodology was based on the belief that the learner would use these beginning experiences at a later time to formulate principles and generalizations on his own.(7) Pestalozzi, a follower of Rousseau, urged teachers to take their pupils out of the classrooms:

> Lead your child out into nature, teach him on the hilltops and in the valleys. There he will listen better, and the sense of freedom will give him more strength to overcome difficulties. But in these hours of freedom let him be taught by nature rather than by you. Let him fully realize that she is the real teacher and that you, with your art, do nothing more than walk quietly at her side.(12)

Other philosophers who embraced the cause of "learning by doing" ranged from Johann Friedrich Herbart (1776-1841) and Herbert Spencer (1820-1903) in the 19th Century, to philosopher-educators John Dewey (1859-1952), Alfred North Whitehead (1861-1947), William Heard Kilpatrick (1871-1965), and William James (1842-1910) in the 20th Century.

The Influence of Contemporary Educational Philosophy

In *Aims of Education*, the "joy of learning" was a theme advocated by Whitehead. Firsthand experiences were essential in dealing with the "real facts." One of his mathematical problems involved surveying a field, making a scale drawing, and finding the area.(13)

John Dewey served as the administrator of one of the first campus laboratory schools in the nation at the University of Chicago. During this experience he authored two books. In *School and Society* (1899), he wrote, ". . . we cannot overlook the importance for educational purposes of the close and intimate acquaintance with nature at first hand . . ." He continued, "No number of object-lessons, got up as object-lessons for the sake of giving information, can afford even the shadow of a substitute for acquaintance with the plants and animals of the farm and garden acquired through actual living among them, and caring for them."(4) Dewey believed quite strongly that every school should be a miniature community that would be imbued with art, history, and science. In the ideal situation, he claimed, "The life of the child would extend out of doors to the garden, surrounding fields and forests. He would have his excursions, his walks and talks, in which the larger world out of doors would open to him."(4)

In *The Child and the Curriculum* (1902), Dewey advocated that experiences of all kinds should be included in the curriculum. Educators should know how to utilize the child's surroundings—physical, natural, social—in a manner that would result in significant learning experiences. Dewey sought to free the learner and the schools from the traditional educational practices of the time. He worked to unify the apparent separation of school and society, learning and doing, and the child and the curriculum. He believed that if the curriculum were more closely related to the child's daily life in his community, dealing with realistic concerns that were important to him, a natural correlation would take place among the various subject matter areas.(5)

In 1900 a series of lectures by William James was published as *Talks to Teachers and Students*. James believed that firsthand experiences were basic to learning when he stated, "The more different kinds of things a child thus gets to know by treating and handling them, the more confident grows his sense of himself with the world in which he lives."

William Heard Kilpatrick, in the third lecture of a series that was published in 1926 under the title, *Education for a Changing Civilization*, stated:

> When we consider the kind of school demanded, three things stand out. First, it must be a school of life, of actual experiencing. Second, it must be a place where pupils are active, where pupil enterprises form the typical unit of learning procedure, for purposeful activity is the typical unit of the worthy life whenever lived. Third, there must be teachers who . . . see and know that growing is growing only as it leads to ever widening effectual control . . .(8)

Kilpatrick believed that experience consisted of both an active and passive side, and that both are necessary and beneficial in the teaching-learning process. However, one reaches his highest living in active experience. The new schools, he urged, must provide this active experience, because the growing use of such experience is both end and means to an end.

In a section labelled "The New Curriculum," Kilpatrick offers a new conception of curriculum as being made up of school experiences that will contribute to the continuous reconstruction of experience. In the old curriculum, subject matter was given back; while in the new curriculum, the learner is "actively at work needing for his present experiences better ways of behaving." Kilpatrick also believed that the most educative of all school activities was when teachers and pupils worked together on unsolved problems.

In response to the question, "How does learning take place?" Kilpatrick advocated three rules:

> First, what we would learn we must practice . . .
> A second rule is . . . we do not learn everything
> we practice. We learn only what succeeds . . . yet
> another condition of learning demands actual
> experiencing in the social situation. This has to do
> with the hope that application will be made of
> what is learned.(8)

Many of these early philosophies and concepts were manifested in the camping education practices that emerged during the pre-1930 period.

Pre-1930 Events

Recognition has already been granted to Frederick W. Gunn for establishing the first organized camp in America in 1861. This two-week summer camp was established at Milford-on-the-Sound in conjunction with the curriculum at the Gunnery School. It appears, however, that the first American school venture in an outdoor setting occurred earlier at Round Hill School between 1823 and 1824.

> Round Hill School was established by George
> Bancroft and Joseph Cogswell. These two Harvard
> graduates sponsored outdoor education, camping,
> and hiking in the form of annual trips to see places
> and things, and geologic expeditions and fishing
> and trapping trips.(9)

Few would question the fact that school camping grew out of the organized camping movement. This pre-1930 period, between the early 1800s, when camps were first organized, until the 1930s, might be identified as the Period of Transition—a time when the variety of programs in organized camping paved the way for the acceptance of school camping programs on the part of both the public and the professional educator.

Another educational innovation that flourished during the early 1900s that claimed support from the same philosophical sources as school camping was the nature study movement. This development is worthy of mention because much of the methodology utilized in current resident outdoor education programs grew out of these earlier endeavors.

Liberty Hyde Bailey (1858-1954) in *The Nature Study Idea*, claimed that this movement began to take form between 1884 and 1890. Louis Agassiz (1807-1873), is recognized by Bailey as being the first scientist to take his students into the field.(22) "Study nature, not books," was his motto. "Agassiz's greatest contribution to American nature study was made by his summer school for teachers."(9)

One of Agassiz's students, H. H. Straight, taught natural science at Oswego Normal School in 1878. This institution was already greatly influenced by the philosophy of object teaching. By taking his classes into the field, Straight also helped promote the concept of correlated studies and teaching about living things in the natural environment.

Nature study education flourished at Cornell University under the leadership of Bailey between 1895 and 1910. The Cornell Nature Study Bulletins appeared during this period; and Anna Botsford Comstock published *The Handbook of Nature-Study* in 1914. It was in this same year that William Gould Vinal (1881-1976) had chronological ties with Mrs. Comstock and the American Nature Study Society. (For a more detailed account of "Cap'n Bill" and his contributions, see Chapter 2.)

© Donald Rettew

Other events that were significant in setting the stage for the next period of camping education were:

1912 - Dubuque (Iowa) Public Schools established a camp for malnourished children.

1918 - Older pupils from the McKinley Avenue Intermediate School in Los Angeles worked on developing a camp site. The project of clearing the ground and constructing a crude log cabin began in 1913 and finished in 1918. This mountain camp was used by the students during vacation periods as well as during school time.(2)

1919 - Chicago Public Schools sponsored a camp that was financed by the Board of Education as part of the regular school program.(11)

1925 - A camp that was used primarily for the demonstration and application of proper forest management techniques and conservation principles for high school youth was established at Clear Creek as a cooperative program between the U.S. Forest Service and the Los Angeles City Schools.(3)

Alcott F. Elwell's dissertation in 1925 was early evidence that indicated that the public schools had started to show an interest in the educational potentialities of the summer camp. After an examination of various societal factors, including the schools, he developed a philosophical case for the "School of the Open" that fulfilled the objectives of the new social philosophy based upon a camping program. Elwell emphasized that there was a difference between his School of the Open, which was a camp where the goals were educational, and those summer camps that were primarily for "amusement." He stressed actual experience and cooperative group effort in a simple natural setting.(14)

Donald Hammerman summarized the Pre-1930 era by stating:

Early developments in outdoor education were, for the most part, isolated experiences carried on nearly as much in the name of recreation as for the purposes of education. The stage was gradually being set, however, for what would ultimately become a clearly defined movement in education; and, in fact, affect teacher education itself. All that was lacking were the proper conditions to initiate a re-examination of educational objectives. These conditions were soon to be met.(7)

The book, *Camping and Character*, by Hedley S. Dimock and Charles E. Hendry, was one of these steps that help provide experimental evidence of the social and moral values that might be gained as the result of a camping experience. In this study, the researchers attempted to determine the changes that occurred in the character traits of boys during a summer camp experience. Their findings provided some indication that one specific camp program could develop certain attitudes and appreciations.(6)

As predicted by Dimock and Hendry, educators in the next decade did become more aware of the educational values of a camping experience in relation to the school curriculum. The Period of Transition ended, and led to the Period of Inception, 1930-1939.

Selected References

1. Bailey, L. H., *The Nature Study Idea*. New York: The MacMillan Co., 1920.
2. Burns, Arthur C., "A Study in Character Building," Unpublished master's thesis, University of Southern California, 1918.
3. California State Department of Education, "Camping and Outdoor Education in California," *Bulletin of the California State Department of Education*, March, 1952.
4. Dewey, John, *The School and Society*, Chicago: The University Chicago Press, 1959.
5. Dewey, John, *The Child and the Curriculum*, Chicago: The University of Chicago Press, 1959.
6. Dimock, Hedley S. and Charles E. Hendry, *Camping and Character*, New York: Association Press, 1929.
7. Hammerman, Donald R., "An Historical Analysis of the Socio-Cultural Factors that Influenced the Development of Camping Education," Unpublished doctoral dissertation, The Pennsylvania State University, 1961.
8. Kilpatrick, William Heard, *Education for a Changing Civilization*, New York: The MacMillan Co., 1927.
9. Lewis, Charles A. Jr., "Factors Influencing the Development of Outdoor Education," Unpublished doctoral dissertation, New York University, 1968.
10. Meyer, Adolph E., *The Development of Education in the Twentieth Century*, Englewood Cliffs: Prentice-Hall, Inc., 1956.
11. Ready, Maria M., *Camps and Public Schools*, Washington, D.C.: U.S. Department of Interior, Office of Education Circular #74, 1933.
12. Ulanoff, Stanley M., "The Origin and Development of Organized Camping in the United States, 1861-1961," Unpublished doctoral dissertation, New York University, 1968.
13. Whitehead, Alfred N., *The Aims of Education*, New York: The MacMillan Co., 1929.
14. Wiener, Morris, "Developing a Rationale for Outdoor Education," Unpublished doctoral dissertation, Michigan State University, 1965.

Chapter 1

OVERVIEW: IMPACT ON AMERICAN EDUCATION

FIFTY YEARS OF RESIDENT OUTDOOR EDUCATION: 1930-1980

by William M. Hammerman and Donald R. Hammerman

William M. Hammerman, Ed.D.
Professor of Education, and
Coordinator, ECO Education Programs
San Francisco State University

William M. Hammerman has spent over twenty-five years teaching elementary through graduate school students from Maryland, Indiana, and Illinois to California. He has conducted numerous N.D.E.A. workshops for teaching science and conservation education in the out-of-doors, served as a consultant to school districts interested in developing outdoor school programs, and has implemented unique resident outdoor education programs for Peace Corps training, disadvantaged youth, and both pre- and in-service teachers. Dr. Hammerman has made several contributions to professional journals and has co-authored *Teaching in the Outdoors* and *Outdoor Education: A Book of Readings*.

Like many outdoor educators, Bill's introduction to this field was through organized summer camp programs. He has worked in resident camp settings for over twenty years serving in positions from "pearl diver" (dishwasher) to director. As Coordinator of Outdoor Education at San Francisco State University, he spent twelve seasons as director of Camp Leonard, an outdoor education center and field campus in the Sierra Nevada.

Dr. Hammerman is a past-president for the Association for Environmental and Outdoor Education, and was the recipient of its Howard Bell Award in 1970. He is a past chairman of the Council on Outdoor Education and Camping, and has received an "Award of Merit" from the American Association for Conservation Information for his contributions to conservation curriculum development and teacher training programs. Bill has been a member of the Task Force on Environmental Education for the National Education Association, and has served as the national coordinator for the American Camping Association's Camp Ecological Training Program. Currently, he is the president of two foundations: the Institute for Environmental, Camping and Outdoor Education, and the Foundation for the Advancement of Environmental Education.

In order for the various "theme" chapters that follow to find their "niche" in that vast mosaic labelled "Fifty Years of Resident Outdoor Education," this introductory, overview chapter attempts to identify and organize the historical developments and the impact of this unique curricular innovation, from 1930-1980, into various transitional periods. Once again, the research literature provided much of the basic information presented in this chapter, and the sources are identified.

Ulanoff, in his historical study of organized camping, quotes a 1924 reference that exemplifies the emergence of outdoor education on the American educational scene:

The history of practically every great movement expressive of human interests, desires and needs, indicates that it passes through several stages in its development. Some person—or at most a very few persons—have an idea, or vision, and proceed either to express this idea or vision in some concrete manner . . . In time the idea spreads and through successive experiences a body of knowledge and tradition comes to exist. An increasing number of people come to possess this knowledge and tradition more from practical experience and through an exchange of experiences with one another. After a time, especially, if the movement draws large numbers of people into it, and the need for leadership correspondingly increases, special training courses and schools become an imperative necessity.(33)

The Period of Inception: 1930-1939

This period was the idea stage of school camping. Camping education was written about and discussed, but little direct action took place. A few forward-looking school systems sponsored summer camp programs. School people, on the whole, were not quite ready to support the idea of camping on school time. A major breakthrough for camping education, however, was a general recognition among educators of the educational values inherent in the summer experience.

Bernard S. Mason's study, *Camping and Education*, published in 1930, represented one of the first attempts to conduct research on camping from a sociological viewpoint. Mason maintained that camping was not either recreation or education; but rather, they were one and the same. He used the four basic "elemental wishes" proposed by William I. Thomas—security, response, recognition, and new experience—as a framework for camping.(18)

As others had done, Mason viewed the camp setting as a miniature segment of the larger society, but still subject to the same forces and dynamics found in any society. He believed that youth had a basic desire for new experiences and his study showed how a camp program could take advantage of this striving for activity on the part of children. Mason concluded that "any adequate approach to camping problems must rest upon an understanding of camper interests."(37)

Lloyd B. Sharp's dissertation, "Education and the Summer Camp—An Experiment," is also widely recognized as one of the earlier significant studies in the development of outdoor education. In his analysis of Sharp's contributions, Wiener stated:

Sharp like others saw a relationship between the goals of education as outlined by Dewey and Kilpatrick and the possibilities inherent in the camp environment . . . He sought to apply the "new educational philosophy" in analyzing a program of welfare agency camping . . . Sharp's concern at this point was not for public education, but like many camping leaders of the time, he was trying to relate broad educational values to that program with which he was most immediately involved.(37)

Although Sharp did not make any references to school camping in his early work, he did recognize that "camping is a series of purposeful, related experiences in real life situations, and is therefore an educational process."(37)

Again, in 1935, Sharp recommended that the recreational needs of people could be served by community-centered schools:

Camping activities should be made part of the regular school program. There is much of educational value in the camp program which the school should utilize. Every school center should have its camps. These camps could operate year-round. The school program could be arranged on some stagger plan so that the school buildings and the camps, and the other facilities, would be in use at all times.(25)

Several other documents that contributed to the impact of the educational use of camping included: Joshua Liberman's *Creative Camping* (1931); "The Summer Camp: A Contribution to Education," by F. Joseph McAuliffe (1934); Carlos W. Ward's *Organized Camping and Progressive Education* (1935); "The Individualization of Large Group Camping" by Ernest

G. Osborne (1936); and Louis H. Blumenthal's *Group Work in Camping* (1937).

It is obvious that, even in this Period of Inception, "the ideas and concepts supporting and defining the movement developed from several sources or points of view." The outdoor education movement, as it is known today, was not easily recognizable as "outdoor education" per se, but resulted from the work of people in such fields as camping, education, recreation, physical education, social welfare, natural science and conservation.(37)

The *Phi Delta Kappan* issue of December, 1938, devoted entirely to camping education, was further evidence of the impact being made by this "frontier" movement upon the American educational scene at this time.(23) In this special issue, just before the close of this period, Jackson R. Sharman was quite definitive in the role that schools should play in the future of education and camping:

> The public school is the agency that should assume the major part of the burden of organizing and operating camps. The objectives of camping are primarily educational and recreational and, therefore, fall appropriately in the sphere of the responsibilities of school boards. It is certain that the schools must accept promptly this new responsibility. Otherwise society will create some new public agency to handle the problem of camping that would probably not be as well qualified as the schools . . . the public schools are the best equipped and best qualified agency for providing this form of education and recreation for all the children of all the people.

As part of the same "editorial comment," Raleigh Schorling was farsighted when he stated, "In all probability the educationist of the year 2000 A.D. will look back upon us and wonder why we, the school people of 1938, failed to include the camp as an integral unit of our educational system."(23)

During the Period of Inception, a few school systems did attempt to broaden their curricula through camping. The U.S. Office of Education reported in a bulletin entitled, "Camping and Outdoor Experiences in the School Program," that since 1930, at Central Washington's College of Education, pupils in the fifth through eighth grades have had a day and a half of camping as a regular feature of their summer session.(17)

William G. Vinal, a renowned nature educator, described the school camp in 1936 as a "laboratory for life" and a "school of realism." He said, "the materials of camp are the materials of life." Vinal's rationale for camping education reflected the influence of John Dewey when he advocated the school camp as an ideal laboratory for subject matter to grow out of experience, rather than experience out of subject matter.(31)

Students attending State Teachers College at Cortland (New York) in 1937 had the opportunity to register for an outdoor leadership training course. Women majoring in physical education were required to attend a two-week training camp in June that included students from Syracuse University.

In 1939, the Highline Public Schools of Washington sponsored a summer camping program for fifth and sixth graders. Their program content, with an emphasis on recreation and camping skills, was typical of the early school ventures in camping. A few pilot programs of this period stressed the civic and social values of the experience. School-operated camps felt the need to promote and preserve the democratic ideal. The school camp was described by one author as a "junior republic," where children would develop into good citizens by becoming active and responsible members of their own small community.(5)

In this initial period, the schools were impacted by a new dimension in education. There was general recognition of the educational benefits of a camping program. The camp experience was viewed as an adjunct to the school program, to be operated primarily during the summer months, not as part of the normal school program. Very few attempts, if any, were made during the Period of Inception to correlate the outdoor learning activities to the regular curriculum. The camp activities, for the most part, were patterned after the traditional summer camp activities: nature study, campcraft, aquatics, hiking, and horseback riding. The aims and goals of these early summer school camps were influenced by the prevailing educational philosophy that the schools should educate for living; consequently, the socialization and the work experiences of camp living were stressed. With the growing acceptance of camping's value to education, the climate was right for the next phase—a period of experimentation.

The Period of Experimentation: 1940-1951

The sponsorship of a national workshop and the development of a community school camp program in 1940, by the W. K. Kellogg Foundation, heralded the beginning of the Period of Experimentation. This experimental program was conducted at the Foundation's camp on Clear Lake. Groups of ninety children from the fifth, sixth, and seventh grades rotated every two weeks throughout the academic year. The program centered around four themes: work experience, healthful living, social living, and leisure pursuits.(19) The theme of the national workshop conducted at Clear Lake Camp was "The Role of Camping in America Today."

Experimentation with school camping was indicative of a general desire to improve school programs through new approaches to curriculum planning. Helen K. Mackintosh stated in the 1947 U.S. Office of Education Bulletin that, "Camping can give the traditional school program a rejuvenation by taking education into the open whenever the out-of-doors can make an experience more real and vital." "Furthermore," she stated, "camping can help to bring about a re-examination of current curriculum practices . . . and (can) develop in simple, direct fashion the practices of democratic living."(17)

In the Foreword to *Public School Camping*, Paul Hanna characterized school camping during this period as ". . . an important innovation on the educational front." Hanna identified two basic values for school camping: (a) providing a number of the ". . . most elementary and fundamental relationships of men to nature and men to men"; and (b) rendering "valuable service to the conservation and improvement of our vast natural resources."(3)

In addition to the Kellogg efforts, other experimental programs were initiated at various grade levels and in all parts of the nation.

1940 - New York State Teachers College at Fredonia initiated a school camping program.

1942 - A ten-day institute for faculty members and students of the New York State Teachers Colleges was conducted at National Camps Life Camps, Inc.

1945 - Clear Lake Camp was the site for a five-year experiment to determine more effective ways to train teachers through camping. This project was a cooperative venture between Western Michigan College of Education and the W. K. Kellogg Foundation.

1946 - The City and County of San Diego launched California's pilot program in outdoor education at Camp Cuyamaca.

1947 - City of Salisbury, North Carolina, experimented with school-sponsored summer camping.

1947 - The New York City experiment signaled an effort to justify the benefits of camping education in terms of school achievement. A detailed description of this experimental design is reported in *Extending Education Through Camping*.

1948 - Cleveland Heights School conducted the first resident outdoor education program in Ohio at Red Raider Camp.

1948 - A seventh grade class from the Demonstration School of the George Peabody College for Teachers in Tennessee participated in a week-long school camping program. The education department and students majoring in education provided the leadership.

1948 - Twelve experimental secondary-level school camp programs were started in Michigan through the cooperation of the W. K. Kellogg Foundation and the State Department of Public Instruction.

1948 - Archer M. Huntington gave the Camp Pine Knot property on Raquette Lake to the New York State Teachers College at Cortland. (Later renamed Huntington Memorial Camp.) Campus school children attended first outdoor education camp.

1949 - Camp Tyler, Texas, began operation under the direction of Dr. George Donaldson. This facility was the first in the nation to be designed specifically as a year-round outdoor laboratory for community-school purposes.

1950 - A one-week work-study camp experiment was conducted for high school boys and girls from Highline, Washington. A film, "Classroom in the Cascades," made possible by a grant from the W. K. Kellogg Foundation, documents the development of this pilot effort.

As school camping began to spread to various parts of the nation during this period, several more professional educational journals recognized this growing impact by publishing special issues: *The School Executive* (February, 1945); *The Bulletin of the National Association of Secondary School Principals* (May, 1947); *The National Elementary Principal* (1949); *The*

Journal of Educational Sociology (May, 1950); and *Education* (September, 1952).

The impact of school camping during the Period of Experimentation was characterized by curriculum emphasis on conservation education, healthful living, meaningful work experiences, socialization, group guidance, and democratic living. Many experimental pilot efforts led to permanent school camping programs. A few administrators saw the participation of the schools in school camping during the summer as a means of extending the school year to a twelve-month program.

The pattern of school-sponsored summer camps, where children could "rough it," were short lived. By the close of this period, most school camps were operating during the regular academic year. In addition, there was a gradual transition from a recreation-centered, camp type program toward a closer relationship with the existing school curriculum.

The Period of Standardization: 1952-1960

The very rapid expansion of school camping across the country was indicative of the impact being made in the educational sector. A gradual move away from a camping stereotype toward a program more closely identified with the school's courses of study was characteristic of this period. Starting in the latter part of the Period of Experimentation, this trend continued to gain wider acceptance during the Period of Standardization. Accompanying this move was a change in nomenclature; there was a general tendency to drop the use of the words "camp" and "camping." Terminology such as "outdoor school," "outdoor laboratory," and "school-in-the-woods" began to appear.

Another major characteristic of this period was the use of manuals, guides, and handbooks. These materials had been developed by various school systems to aid classroom teachers in planning for the outdoor school experience. These manuals tended to bring an element of standardization and uniformity to the school camping experience.

In St. Clair's analysis of ninety-two schools that sponsored resident outdoor education programs, she concluded that the activity curriculum tended to prevail as the identified education curriculum philosophy (i.e., "A curriculum in which the content and structure are determined by the interests and needs of the children as they defined them. Subject matter is used to fulfill the purposes and aspirations of the students.") However, nearly as many schools identified the core curriculum as the basis for their program (i.e., "A curriculum in which a core of social values is emphasized. It is structured around broad social problems or themes of living. It is typified by teacher-pupil planning, but it tends to adhere more to a principle of basic organization than does the activity curriculum. Skills are taught as they are needed.") She also observed that school camps had remained an extension of the classroom, they had not become an omnibus of the outdoors.(29)

The creation of organizations and the formulation of standards are indications that an educational movement has matured. The Outdoor Education Association was established in 1951 and incorporated two years later. In California, the Association for Outdoor Education was founded in 1954. The American Association for Health, Physical Education and Recreation, a Department of the National Education Association, appointed a task force in 1954 to formulate, judge, and approve a set of standards for public school camping. The committee's final product contained standards for camp objectives, camp membership, camp leadership, camp program, and the profession.(28)

Further impact by organizations was felt when a national Outdoor Education Project was initiated in 1955. Although the primary purpose of this project was the promotion of outdoor recreational activities, the various workshops conducted by the project did aid in the dissemination of information pertaining to resident outdoor education. At the end of the project's third year, over 3,500 school personnel had participated in workshops conducted in twenty-eight states.(27)

The first National Conference on Outdoor Education was held in Washington, D.C. in May, 1958. This event, also sponsored by the American Association for Health, Physical Education and Recreation, attracted 125 school and college administrators and teachers, conservationists, industrialists, recreationalists, and representatives of professional organizations and governmental agencies.(26) The final sessions were devoted to two fundamental issues in outdoor education: (a) teacher and leadership preparation for outdoor education; and (b) school programs in camp settings.

As this period ended, school camping—although playing a central role—was being viewed as one aspect of the total spectrum of outdoor education programs. National organizations recognized the impact of the school camping movement by creating separate sub-units in their structures, and sponsoring programs devoted to outdoor education at their regional and national conventions. For example, the American Camping Association created a School Camping Committe in 1956. ACA sponsored a consultation on School Camping and Outdoor Education from January 8-10,

1959, at its headquarters at Bradford Woods, Indiana. Interest groups were formulated around topics such as: facilities needed by school groups; terminology—clarification of terms; and leadership development and training.

The Period of Resurgence and Innovation: 1960-1969

In comparison to previous periods, the next decade is difficult to label as far as developments pertaining to "resident" outdoor education. As this educational concept continued to spread, it became impossible for any one individual, association, project, or organization to keep track of all the trends and developments. The field of outdoor education continued to diversify. The emphasis of various programs ranged from pre-school children to graduate students; from short, local field trips to cross-country expeditions; and from outdoor recreation skills to ecological studies.

The values of resident outdoor education continued to have an impact on the school sector. With the increased use of the out-of-doors as a laboratory for learning for pre-service and in-service teachers, the first National Outdoor Teacher Education Conference was held at Northern Illinois State College's Lorado Taft Field Campus in 1960. Several outdoor education books appeared in the "academic marketplace" which included chapters dealing with the need for resident programs: *Philosophy of Outdoor Education* (1961) and *Programs in Outdoor Education* (1962) by William Freeberg and Loren Taylor; *Teaching in the Outdoors* (1964) by Hammerman and Hammerman, followed by their *Outdoor Education: A Book of Readings* (1968); *Outdoor Education* (1963) by Smith, Carlson, Donaldson and Masters; *The Role of Outdoor Education* (1965) by Gabrielson and Holtzer; *Outdoor Education* (1967) by Charles Mand; and Walter Schramm's *Classroom Out-of-Doors* (1969).

A Second National Conference on Outdoor Education was held in 1962 at the Gull Lake Biological Station in Michigan. The main theme centered around the general relationship between outdoor education and fitness and leisure to "education in and for the outdoors and the specific implications of the Report of the Outdoor Recreation Resources Review Commission in Education."(24) The American Association for Health, Physical Education and Recreation organized the Council on Camping and Outdoor Education in 1965.

The Association for Outdoor Education dedicated its tenth annual conference, in 1964, to Dr. L. B. Sharp "who devoted his life to the vision of education in the out-of-doors. The conference theme was, "Man and His Relationship to Nature."

The most significant development in outdoor education during this decade, however, resulted from the passage of the Elementary and Secondary Education Act of 1965. Its basic purpose was "to strengthen and improve educational quality and educational opportunities in the Nation's elementary and secondary schools." Charles Lewis wrote that the portion of this legislation (Title III) which pertained to the creation of supplementary centers and services, had a major impact on the growth and development of outdoor education programs in the United States. Within the ESEA guidelines, one specific funding possibility mentioned under Title III that the U.S. Office of Education suggested was summer or year-round camping. Over a two-year period, 1966 and 1967, more than five million dollars was spent on eighty-nine projects involving outdoor education. Several of these projects were resident centers and the programs included the study of natural resources, weather, astronomy, ecology, conservation, mathematics, and physical fitness.(13)

Northern Illinois University

In his study Lewis briefly described seventy-three PACE outdoor education projects funded in thirty-five states with Title III monies. He also identified the following common denominators:(13)

1 - The various projects made use of the out-of-doors environment as an extension of the classroom for certain educational experiences that take place best in a teaching situation which is removed from the school building.

2 - A resident experience was utilized—the school camp or the outdoor education center—for the advancement of human development, inter-personal relationships, and in-depth curriculum related experiences.

3 - In-service training experiences were instituted to acquaint teaching and administrative personnel with techniques for using the out-of-doors.

4 - The outdoor education method was utilized for studying pollution topics and for aesthetic experiences.

In his concluding remarks regarding the final status of the impact on the growth and development of out-door education that had been made by the Elementary and Secondary Education Act, Lewis stated:

It is apparent that Title III funds will have done much to enable districts and regions to explore the educational possibilities offered through outdoor education. The key to measured success under Title III will be the extent to which outdoor education is adopted on an on-going basis as part of the regular curriculum in those districts which have received Federal aid.(13)

Another Federal development that had an impact on the provision of facilities for outdoor education experiences was the announcement in 1963 by President John F. Kennedy that the Tennessee Valley Authority would have the responsibility of planning and developing a demonstration area in Western Kentucky and Tennessee for outdoor educational and recreational facilities. One of the areas, the Land Between the Lakes, included a specific facility—the Youth Activities Station—that provided accommodations for resident programming. The original "Land Between the Lakes Concept Statement" indicated that the area "will serve as a laboratory for students and educators working in the field of recreation and camping education."(12)

Eight years after the first National Conference on Outdoor Education, a third was held in Washington, D.C., in 1966. Attendance doubled that of the second conference in 1962. The tone for the conference was set by Hugh B. Masters in his keynote talk, "Outdoor Education—A Need of the Times."(30) According to Lewis, the pre-conference session devoted to the concern of the role of Federal aid in "supporting program growth in outdoor education and the pressing need to develop adequate guidelines and procedures for evaluating outdoor education programs" was of particular significance. Lewis concluded that this National Conference was a turning point in the growth and development of outdoor education in the United States; he labeled this event as the "Coming of Age of Outdoor Education."(13)

A quite visible dimension during the 1960s was the circulation of numerous newsletters that enabled outdoor educators to share current information. The first national magazine in the field, *The Journal of Outdoor Education*, published its pilot issue in 1966.(6)

A resurgence of interest in outdoor education and camping education took place during this period, along with financial support provided by the Federal Government. Since this decade saw new directions and dimensions identified for outdoor education, it must also be recognized that—up to now—not too much had been done in the field of resident programming for special populations: the retarded, the handicapped, and the emotionally disturbed.

Campbell Loughmiller's *Wilderness Road* was published in 1965. He described a residential program for boys whose difficulties required treatment outside the home. Camp Woodland Springs was largely experimental and served underprivileged boys during the summer months and on weekends during the remainder of the year. Every boy admitted to the camp had experienced failure in school; many were also emotionally handicapped. Seventy percent made satisfactory adjustment in the post-camp period. An additional twenty-four percent made appreciable gains that enabled them to function at a significant higher level." Although academic achievement was considered important, the major purpose of the camp program was to help the boys achieve a better personality integration in order to function more effectively in various situations.(15)

In the mid-1960s, the Outdoor Education Center for San Francisco State College was utilized as a "field training site" for Peace Corps Volunteers going to Liberia as teachers. During this one-week session, at the end of their on-campus training, the trainees were divided into decentralized, primitive camping groups. In addition to the normal campcraft skills, these future teachers learned how to teach math, science, art, geography, history, and language arts in the out-of-doors.(10)

Some of the ideas generated in the Peace Corps training program were carried over to a Title I, ESEA summer school program that was funded by various California school districts from 1966 through 1971. During the camp sessions, classroom teachers served as teacher-counselors who lived and worked with respective groups. Although the majority of children served were fifth and sixth graders, a variety of program models were developed for grades two through twelve. Regardless of the particular program format selected, the basic goals of this resident outdoor laboratory and living experience for disadvantaged youth were: (11)

1 - To promote healthier human relations.

2 - To increase the motivation to want to learn.

3 - To improve communication skills.

4 - To develop an appreciation and understanding of our natural resources.

5 - To help prepare teachers to work more effectively with culturally disadvantaged youth.

During the latter portion of this period, an old theme in many outdoor education programs—the relationship of man to his environment—took on new significance and priority in the world of education. Environmental education programs interacted with outdoor education programs and each was influenced by the other. In some instances, the name of a resident program was simply changed from outdoor education to environmental education. The new definition was now, "Education *in* the environment, *for* the environment, and *about* the environment."

In 1967, Project NEED (National Environmental Education Development) was initiated in order to develop "an appreciation and critical environmental awareness among Americans through an understanding of the natural and cultural interactions illustrated in the areas" administered by the National Park Service.(8)

The first phase of the NEED program emphasized an encounter at an outdoor school site that focused on aesthetic and physical relationships with the natural order. The various experiences were developed around a conceptual framework that consisted of the following strands: similarities and differences; patterns; interaction and interdependence; continuity and change. The total program gradually involved a complete K-12 package with one day—or shorter—excursions. The intent of the NEED program was to prepare material that augmented the present school curricula.

The U.S. Forest Service developed an experiential centered series of environmental investigations, with the help of teachers, between 1968-1971. Many residential centers utilized this collection of field investigations that focused on a process approach and problem solving approach to learning. Within this "Investigating Your Environment" package are lesson plans that investigate the soil, water, forest, and urban environments by involving the participant in collecting, recording, and interpreting data. Other activities involve simulation games, measuring the environment, and investigating an environmental issue.

Although renewed interest was developed in school camping, broader and newer horizons were the characteristics of this decade. The expanded terminology and the diversity of program emphasis in the latter portion of the 1960s was to continue and to merge with the next phase—The Period of New Directions.

Period of New Directions: 1970-1979

More than 100 leaders attended the Fourth National Conference on Outdoor Education at Hickory Corners, Michigan, during October, 1970. "The World of Outdoor Education: Issues—Problems—Challenges" was the theme for this event, once again sponsored by the Outdoor Education Project and the Council on Outdoor Education and Camping. Throughout this decade, the Council sponsored six more conferences: the International Conference at Dorset, Canada (1972); Estes Park, Colorado (1974) with the theme, "Plains to Peak Top"; Isabellea, Minnesota (1976) with the theme, "Experiential Education in Snow Country"; Rogersville, Alabama (1977) with the theme, "Appalachia: Yesterday, Today, and Tomorrow"; Carefree, Arizona (1978) with the theme, "From the Desert to the Alpine"; and Lake Placid, New York (1979) with the theme, "An Olympiad of Outdoor Education Recreation and Wilderness Adventure."

The resurgence of interest in utilizing the out-of-doors as a learning laboratory and the creation of innovative applications of the concept of outdoor education in the previous period, led to a larger sphere of influence as new directions became established in educational practices.

Environmental Education. Environmental education continued to be a major thrust of many resident outdoor education programs in the new decade. Three events that represented this nation's concern for the environment were Earth Day I (April 22, 1970), the first report of the Council on Environmental Quality (August, 1970), and the passage of the National Environmental Education Act (October, 1970).

Simon Chavez made the obervation that "Americans seem to go from one massive movement to another. Today the call to action is environmental factors . . . The problem of environmental factors is not one in which the environment is a problem." As with most environmental crises, it is man who has become a problem to the environment; and in the long run, a threat to himself. This situation is, in part, a problem for education; it is essential that the learner understands the interrelationships that exist between man and his environment. Chavez made his key point, "This calls for provisions for children to learn from reality itself. It calls for a system of learning that is based on experience, on inquiry, on discovery, and on analysis. It is a system that involves the whole child; his affective, physical, cognitive, and aesthetic nature. It calls for outdoor education."(2)

A report from the Educational Facilities Laboratories (1972), developed in cooperation with the National Education Association and the National Park Service, recognized the impact of resident programs as one of many approaches to environmental education:

> A one-week resident educational environment-centered camp for fifth and sixth graders is becoming a regular part of many school curriculums. These resident camps started out originally in school camping and outdoor education programs. Many of these programs still maintain the name of outdoor education, but much of what has been incorporated into them today is called environmental education . . . The change in terminology from outdoor education to environmental education seems to be symbolic of the subtle change in emphasis from a focus on the natural environment to a broader consideration of man's total environment, including population, pollution, transportation, etc.(7)

In addition to new themes and topics, the literature began to reflect a return to experience-based learning strategies. Among the most creative applications of these earlier philosophies were the learning approaches espoused by Steve Van Matre in *Acclimatization* (1972), *Acclimatizing* (1974), and *Sunship Earth* (1979). Van Matre stresses a sensory and conceptual approach to ecological involvement. His approach to understanding relationships in the natural world is very personal and reflective. (34, 35, 36)

Starting in 1969, but reaching a peak during America's Bicentennial, students have had the opportunities to recreate the time or culture of their choice in a variety of Environmental Living Programs. These programs are concerned not only with cultural ways of the past, but also with how earlier Americans learned to live in harmony with their natural environment. These resident experiences are essentially learning activities in which youth recreate the past and then find ways in which lessons learned from role-simulations in other eras might be useful in solving future problems. A partial list of California sites sponsoring Environmental Living Programs is representative of a broad range of learning opportunities:

Fort Point National Historic Site—A Civil War military garrison.
Historic Ships—A turn-of-the-century sailor's life on a lumber schooner.
John Muir National Historic Site—Life of a Chinese field hand in the 1880s.
Petaluma Adobe State Historic Park—Life on a California Mexican rancho.
Turlock Lake State Recreational Area—Life of Indians in a Miwok Village.

Adventure Education. Adventure education programs have been an outgrowth of the Outward Bound schools, introduced in the United States in 1962. Utilized primarily at the secondary school level, adventure-based education is an experience of self-discovery that uses challenges in a wilderness setting as the teaching medium. Many institutions, ranging from correctional agencies, Vista, Peace Corps, and Job Corps, to private schools, have adapted the Outward Bound philosophy to their own programs in a variety of patterns. The basic claim for these programs is that a person who experiences self-discovery in the wilderness can transfer the underlying lessons of self-awareness, respect for others, and environmental concerns to other spheres of his life space: school, home, and community.(21)

Many summer camps, as well as resident outdoor education centers, have expanded their offerings to include backpacking, rafting, cycling, and mountain climbing expeditions. Many schools have also developed challenge or "rope courses" for both day and residential use.

Another new direction for the 1970s that was fostered by adventure education programs has been the re-emergence of "action learning" or "experiential education." The Association for Experiential Education was established in 1977. Although the spectrum of learning activities included in this "umbrella" term is broad, it does include resident programs conducted in outdoor settings.

James S. Coleman, in an address to the Sixth Annual Conference on Experiential Education in 1978, made the following statement:

> . . . if experiential learning is to have a strong and secure place in the learning environments of the future, we need a better understanding of just what functions it fulfills . . . we have a poverty of experience in life . . . the household, which was once a productive unit, overrun with people, activity, strife, demands, love, and work . . . has now become antiseptic, a boarding-house where family members come to sleep . . . a place where their paths cross as they go back and forth to their specialized activities.

> The child's specialized activity is the school which acts as a protective shield against the mine, the factory, the farm field, the streets . . . We have intentionally cut off the child's nourishment by experience . . . (4)

Coleman made the same point that outdoor educators have been stating from the beginning, "experiential education has always been with us . . . the task, then, if we are to be serious about designing appropriate environments for children and youth is . . . what do we want experience for?" The main point made through his verbal examples was that in order to achieve the same basic skills that the schools wish to acquire, some forms of experiential learning are essential. Some types of experiential education may lead to self-knowledge, and others might provide direct contact with other lives and settings beyond his own.(4)

Special Populations. Although some program leaders for special population groups have been experimenting with resident outdoor education, environmental education, and adventure education for years, this decade saw the number of outdoor education opportunities available for these groups—as well as adult and senior citizens—increase dramatically.

Project REACH, a three-year (1976-1979) research and development project administered by the University of Kentucky, and funded by the Bureau of Education for the Handicapped, developed competency-based instructional materials designed to improve and expand the quantity and quality of camping services.

A division of the Association for Experiential Education labeled Adventure Alternatives in Corrections, Mental Health and Special Education, was created. One of their initial tasks was to identify programs around the country. A second book by Campbell Loughmiller, *Kids in Trouble*, was published in 1979. Like his earlier work, it emphasized the concepts and practices that were found to be most helpful in achieving an eighty-five per cent success rate with seriously disturbed youth.

The Fund for the Advancement of Camping sponsored a consortium consultation in September, 1979, that dealt with the "state of the art" of alternatives to incarceration for maladaptive children. FAC has been increasingly interested in the need for an interdisciplinary approach to more effective use of outdoor education and organized camping to meet the challenge of an urbanized society and its various special populations. This particular consultation initiated an exploration of outdoor programs as a prevention-intervention model for maladaptive and adjudicated youth. Both stress/challenge and resident camp programs were recognized as having a potential contribution to make in helping maladaptive youth adjust to the urban environment. One outcome was an agreement to cosponsor, with the American Camping Association, a 1980 pre-convention symposium on camping and special populations that would include the physically disabled, mentally disabled, and elderly, in addition to emotionally troubled and delinquent youth.

The Second National/International Outdoor Education Workshop held at the Lorado Taft Field Campus had among its major themes for 1979: curriculum development, environmental awareness, resident programs, cultural history, and outdoor recreation. This period ended in 1979 along with the appearance of *Outdoor Education for the Whole Child* by Frederick A. Staley.

Almost fifty years later, American educators have a "smorgasbord" of programs in outdoor settings from which to choose. The activities and age levels vary, but the essence—the direct experience approach to learning—is the same. In the chapters that follow, three personalities that have had an impact on this field of education are highlighted. In addition, selected topics have been identified, and various outdoor education specialists have addressed themselves to the impact of resident outdoor education on their particular theme.

Selected References

1. Blumenthal, Louis H., *Group Work in Camping*. New York: Association Press, 1937.
2. Chavez, Simon, "Outdoor Education, Dayton Style," in *Outlines of Environmental Education*. Madison: Dembar Education Research Services, Inc., 1971.
3. Clarke, James M., *Public School Camping*. Stanford: Stanford University Press, 1951.
4. Coleman, James S., "Experiential Learning and Information Assimilation: Toward an Appropriate Mix," *The Journal of Experiential Education*, Spring, 1979.
5. Curtis, Henry S., "The School Camp," *Journal of the National Education Association*, April, 1935.
6. Donaldson, George W., and Oswald H. Goering, "Outdoor Education: A Synthesis," ERIC/CRESS publication, New Mexico State University, March, 1970.
7. *Environmental Education/Facility Resources*. New York: Education Facilities Laboratory, 1972.
8. Evison, Boyd, "The National Park System and Environmental Education," in *Outlines of Environmental Education*. Madison: Dembar Educational Research Services, Inc., 1971.
9. Hammerman, Donald R., "An Historical Analysis of the Socio-Cultural Factors that Influenced the Development of Camping Education," Unpublished doctoral Dissertation, The Pennsylvania State University, 1961.
10. Hammerman, William M., "The Peace Corps Goes Camping," *Camp Directors' Digest*, January, 1965.
11. Hammerman, William M. and Richard M. Brians, "Adventure in Learning," *Childhood Education*, October, 1967.
12. *Land Between the Lakes Concept Statement*. Knoxville: The Tennessee Valley Authority, 1964.
13. Lewis, Charles, "Factors Influencing the Development of Outdoor Education," Unpublished doctoral dissertation, New York University, 1968.
14. Lieberman, Joshua, *Creative Camping*. New York: Association Press, 1931.
15. Loughmiller, Campbell, *Wilderness Road*, The Hogg Foundation for Mental Health, The University of Texas, 1965.
16. Loughmiller, Campbell, *Kids in Trouble*. Tyler, Texas: Wildwood Books, 1979.
17. Mackintosh, Helen K., "Camping and Outdoor Experiences in the School Program," Washington, D.C.: Office of Education, Federal Security Agency, Bulletin No. 4, 1947.
18. Mason, Bernard S., *Camping and Education*, New York: The McCall Co., 1930.
19. Masters, Hugh B., "A Community School Camp," *The Elementary School Journal*, June, 1941.
20. McAuliff, F. Joseph, "The Summer Camp: A Contribution to Education," Unpublished doctoral dissertation, Boston College, 1934.
21. Nold, Joseph T., *Outward Bound Approaches to Alternative Schooling*, Colorado Outward Bound School, 1970.
22. Osborne, Ernest G., "The Individualization of Large Group Camping," Unpublished doctoral dissertation, Columbia University, 1936.
23. *Phi Delta Kappan*, Phi Delta Kappa, December, 1938.
24. *Second National Conference on Outdoor Education, A Program Brochure*. Michigan: The Outdoor Education Project, 1962.
25. Sharp, Lloyd B., "Health and Physical Education in a Community Centered School," *Clearing House*, March, 1935.
26. Smith, Julian W., "First National Conference on Outdoor Education," *Journal of Health, Physical Education, Recreation*, October, 1958.
27. Smith, Julian W., "Three Years of Progress: Report of the American Association for Health, Physical Education and Recreation Outdoor Project," *Journal of Health, Physical Education, Recreation*, January, 1959.
28. Squires, John L., "Standards in Public School Camping," *Journal of American Association for Health, Physical Education and Recreation*, September, 1954.
29. St. Clair, Janet, "The Education Curriculum Philosophy of a Select Group of School Camps," Unpublished master's thesis, State University of Iowa, 1958.
30. "Third Conference on Outdoor Education, National Report," *Journal of Health, Physical Education and Recreation*, January, 1967.
31. Vinal, William G., "The School Camp Line-Up for Nature Education," *Clearing House*, April, 1936.
32. Ward, Carlos W., *Organized Camping and Progressive Education*. Nashville: Cullum and Chertner, 1935.
33. Ulanoff, Stanley M., "The Origin and Development of Organized Camping in the United States, 1861-1961," Unpublished doctoral dissertation, New York University, 1968.
34. Van Matre, Steve, *Acclimatization*. Martinsville, Indiana, American Camping Association, 1972.
35. Van Matre, Steve, *Acclimatizing*. Martinsville, Indiana: American Camping Association, 1974.
36. Van Matre, Steve, *Sunship Earth*. Martinsville, Indiana: American Camping Association, 1979.
37. Wiener, Morris, "Developing a Rationale for Outdoor Education," Unpublished doctoral dissertation, Michigan State University, 1965.

Walter Saunders

Chapter 2

CONTRIBUTIONS OF WILLIAM G. VINAL

FIFTY YEARS OF RESIDENT OUTDOOR EDUCATION: 1930-1980

by John W. Brainerd

John W. Brainerd, Ph.D.
Professor of Biology and Conservation
Springfield College, Massachusetts

John W. (Doc) Brainerd was born in the country outside Boston where his childhood experiences brought him in contact with wildlife. At Harvard, he majored in biology and was secretary of the ornithological club. As a graduate student he instigated the first Harvard Ecological Colloquia when "ecology" was still a dirty word among most biologists. A conscientious objector during World War II, Dr. Brainerd served with the U.S. Forest Service and the U.S. Fish and Wildlife Service. After the war, while writing his thesis on "The Vegetation of Dover During Three Hundred Years of White Man's History," he observed his native countryside being suburbanized.

He joined the Biology Department at Springfield College in 1949, specializing in training for community leadership, and promoting environmental understanding in both the city and the country with his students. Dr. Brainerd has worked with many organizations, including the Camp Naturalist Committee of the American Camping Association, was past president for the American Nature Study Society, editor for The Nature Conservancy, and chairman of the Conservation Committee of the National Association of Biology Teachers. He is a Fellow of the American Association for the Advancement of Science and of the Association of Interpretive Naturalists. He holds a life membership with the American Forestry Association and is an honorary life member of the Appalachian Mountain Club.

"Doc" has written many leaflets and articles promoting better use of schoolgrounds, campgrounds, and bikeways. His many poems are signed Jay Bee. He has authored and illustrated two books, *Nature Study for Conservation—A Handbook for Environmental Education,* and *Working with Nature—A Practical Guide.* His filmstrips include "Forests of the Northeast (Autumn and Winter)" and "Shores—The Edges of Things."

Dr. William Gould Vinal was a big man, big in many ways and important to resident outdoor education. By 1930, the beginning of our fifty-year review, he was himself almost fifty, yet with forty influential years ahead in which to touch innumerable campers and camp administrators. One of his biggest assets, so he often said, was the meagerness of his close-to-the-soil child-hood environment. He was born in a 201-year-old Cape Cod farmhouse and was raised on the farm in what he described as poverty. He appreciated his own personal "resident outdoor education" there in a big way.

While he did not take himself too seriously, he revered his forebears, respected his natural and his cultural environments, and gave grave thought to those who would come after him. In 1970, he still seemed in his *first* childhood. Still working as hard as he was able, he had retained his capacity for play. He was cele-brating his November birthday and still writing glowing-ly of his Anglo-Saxon ancestry and the early settlers of Plimoth Plantation harvesting corn, bean, and pumpkin Indian style.

Some wise person said, "The measure of a man is the size of the thing it takes to get his goat,"—meaning to irritate him enough to make him act foolishly. Many people thought Vinal a fool. Why would a grown man in Cleveland, Chicago, or the Rocky Mountains tolerate being called "Cap'n Bill?" That name started on Wellfleet Bay, Cape Cod, Massachusetts, at Camp Chequesset, which he founded in 1914. He recounted, "We decided that our titles had to be informal for a camp situation. The word 'professor' was tabooed . . . I was known as 'Cap'n Bill." That name stuck because he was informally approachable and lovable and because he knew that the camp environment with its simpler ways was basic to all life. To mix metaphors, which he "learly doved" to do. He brought a breath of fresh air with him as a common denominator wherever he went. Only people who had lost perspective felt threatened by his simplicity and called him foolish. They had no scale by which to measure a man so large in stature.

Do you remember how in the 1960s a thing that was in style was termed "camp?" Cap'n Bill did not go in and out of style. He did not have to go back to basics; he was already there. He had a keen appreciation of funda-mentals and recognized that living outdoors necessitates being directly involved with nature and with oneself. Of course, he could put up a false front just for the hell of it; but if you took some pokes at the mask you would always find that Cap'n Bill was Cap'n Bill. He recalled with delight how F. Schuyler Matthews, renowned botanist and ornithologist, came to Camp Chequesset with a dress suit so as to be properly attired for his

evening lecture on bird songs. He soon found he did not need to wear it! Stuffed shirts, Cap'n Bill felt, were an affront to reality.

Dr. Vinal was a big man, hard to pin down. If you stated a fact bluntly, he was apt to question it, demon-strating how partial was your truth. If you asked him a question, he would Socratically ask you another, which if correctly answered would lead you toward answering your own question. Maddening—this technique enabled the wise to become wiser while fools drifted away. And he was a rambler, he was. He liked to take ample time to amble. He would pick up a stone and remind you that "every pebble is a particular one." Similarly he would pick up a word and toy with it. He was a funster; he'd add a jot to the *f* of *funster* and make *punster*. He'd turn a sailing toy around and hand you a sailing yot. If you tried to pin him, he'd nip you. How silly that Billy would pun for fun; but the kids loved it and some educators—not all—would appreciate the method in his madness, realizing that his love of words made him a master of verbal communication and that the love was infectious.

It would be presumptious to try to "explain" Dr. Vinal. He might ask, "How much of me is hereditary and how much environmental?" He'd keep you guessing and teach you much about both, preferably around a campfire. Likewise it is difficult though quite worthwhile to conjecture how this amiable yet forceful person, born humbly and staying humble, influenced resident outdoor education. Let us view him in various situations prior to 1930.

1881-1900: Boyhood on farm doing farm chores, learning of life as member of family caring for soil, plants, and animals. 1900-1903: Bridgewater (Massa-chusetts) Normal School studying to teach, staying as librarian in 1903-1904, thereby keeping in touch with girl friend, to whom he was later married for 63 years ('Mother V, always a helpful partner). 1906: Graduate studies in biology and forestry at Harvard; laboratory assistant in botany. Summer of 1907: Research on *Life History of the Scallop* while living in a fisherman's shack at the southern tip of Cape Cod. 1907-1909: Teaching biology, physiography, and sports at Marshall College, West Virginia, apparently finding great rapport with hill-country youths. Summers 1908-1913: Continuing field research for Massachusetts Division of Fish and Game in Barnstable and Plymouth counties. 1910-1911: Teaching geography at Salem Normal School for a professor on sabbatical leave. Summer 1911: Heading nature study department at Rhode Island Normal School, a position held enthusiastically for fourteen years. "By now I was unpredictable. My inner self was cropping out," he said.

1914-1925: Director of Camp Chequesset, "A nautical camp for knotty girls" on Cape Cod. At Chequesset a fertile mingling of the farmboy background and the academic disciplines of biology and geography in the natural and social surroundings of a resident camp. Vinal was a well-integrated personality giving confident leadership in imaginative ways.

The breadth of his interests is significant. He transcended narrow sciencing. He melded natural sciences with social sciences while getting campers involved in Cape Cod community life through graphic arts, drama, music, church affairs, and contact with inhabitants of Cape Cod as they made their daily livelihoods.

Away back then he was teaching through oral history by having campers visit the elderly. He was teaching communication through presentation of skits and journal writings. He was teaching sensitivity and responsibility and dependability by having each camper who so desired care for a pet animal and a garden plot. The girls and their college-trained counselors and visiting experts were often involved in what is now called nature crafts, largely based on Indian lore.

Straight-line chronology, though, cannot describe Dr. Vinal's development. His autobiographical notes skip and jump, not so much as one might expect from the worn mental gearwheels of one in his nineties, but as one expects from an enthusiastic youngster. For continuing decades his ecological sensitivities webbed his thinking. The strands of his thought processes were not dusty cobwebs but tautly integrated understandings of the complexities of man-nature relationships. So while one can visualize Cap'n Bill teaching girls seamanship and seaweeds on Wellfleet Bay and helping them make campfire skits in dune hollows, one can further realize that World War I and Vinal's work at Rhode Island Normal School were helping him develop his social philosophy on a much broader base than Cape Cod's idyllic camping environment.

The bigness of that philosophy was apparent in his later years, when increasing numbers of people were more willing to listen. Their readiness must have been in large measure a result of the greatness of his energy over many decades. His puritanical work ethic, for instance, made him sit down and write and write. In his Rhode Island years, a major effort produced a series of Arbor Day leaflets. In that period he stressed the importance of winter camping and how tree identification in winter could integrate with outdoor adventures using wood.

In the first two decades of the century, Dr. Vinal became involved with Liberty Hyde Bailey, a Cornell University student of Harvard Asa Gray. Bailey, himself a man of stupenduous energies, evolved *Cornell Rural School Leaflets* to help teachers in rural schools guide youngsters into what we now think of as ecological life-styles. His book *The Nature Study Idea* (1903) had helped launch The American Nature Study Society. Vinal teamed up with Bailey's right-hand helper, Anna Botsford Comstock, to publish a pocket looseleaf manual of nature study that became widely used in camps and normal schools for training teachers and other youth leaders. It gave fingertip stimulus and knowledge for living outdoors and had an unquantifiable influence. By 1916, Vinal had published his "Nature Study in Rhode Island" in *Nature Study Review*. In 1918, the same publication carried his "The Nature Program at Camp Chequesset." In his nineties, Vinal wrote, "I have written more mileage on *camps* (his emphasis) than on any other topic." In 1920, *Nature Study Review* published its first camp number, William Gould Vinal, editor.

For some sixty years, Cap'n Bill fought a personal war against classroom stuffiness. If his spirit today is not cajoling God or Satan into more outdoor activities, at least his remaining essence here on his beloved planet Earth is working hard amidst innumerable former students and colleagues trying to influence the educational system to teach more outdoors and around the clock.

By 1920, Vinal was teaching a course at Teachers College, Columbia University, in New York City; the best part of the course for Vinal was the week at Bear Mountain, where he was camp director with a roster of camping and natural history notables on his staff. His Ph.D. degree came in 1922 from Brown University, with a thesis on *Anomia simplex*, the jingle shell. How appropriate! He could work within the system but always had his fun in the process.

Vinal helped found and then directed the influential Nature Lore School from 1920 to 1928, usually a ten-day course held at Camp Chequesset. Students came from many states and some foreign countries to become better nature leaders, mostly in camps and schools. Recreation as an organized field of human endeavor had been growing fast in the preceding decade; many of his students were interested in the playground movement. The average age of the Nature Lore School students was 28 years.

In the early 1920s, Vinal came solidly into line with the Boy Scouts of America as an Eagle Scout, scoutmaster, commissioner, and later member-at-large of the National Council. Who can measure his influence on this significant camping movement?

The summer of 1922 saw Vinal nature guiding at Yosemite National Park, where Enos Mills had been so influential in starting the western nature guiding. He also attended Boy Scout camp at Estes Park, Colorado camped with Mother V at Glacier National Park, and was a guide again at Crater Lake.

In 1923, the year that *American Nature Magazine* published his article, "The Counselor and the Camp," that magazine and the American Camping Association sponsored Cap'n Bill and Mother V for camp visitations in New York and New England. By 1925, Vinal was elected president of the American Camping Association; and the American Nature Association's first yearbook, edited by E. L. Palmer of Cornell, included a Vinal article on "Teacher Training in Nature Study."

From 1925 to 1927, Vinal was professor of nature study at the New York State College of Forestry at Syracuse in the Department of Forest Extension. There he was recorded as having given 105 talks in 1927, a record number, and was described as a prolific writer. One year he wrote 17 different items for publication, including a 551-page book, *Nature Guiding*. That book is still useful; erudite, yet down to earth.

In 1926, Vinal was speaking at the annual meeting of the American Nature Study Society, of which he later became president. At the National Recreation Congress, his topic was, "The Program of Nature Study for the Recreation System." His national stature was growing fast, yet his work was always close to the earth and to simple folk, as with his article on "What to Do on a Hike" in the June 1929 issue of *Playground*.

In the summer of 1927, Cap'n Bill and Mother V, sponsored by the National Camp Directors' Association and the American Nature Association visited a camp a day in New England and New York. That fall they moved to Cleveland, Ohio, where numerous endeavors centering around his work in the science department of the School of Education at Western Reserve University spread his good influence in Middle America. In 1928 and 1929, he directed a nature lore school for the Izaak Walton League of America, a venture similar to the training sessions he had had for ten-day periods at Camp Chequesset. From 1928 to 1935, he directed a nature guide school for Western Reserve University for six weeks each summer. It offered a course for credit, complete with two groups of children for the teachers in training. The Junior Nature Guides were resident campers and the Nature Guard was composed of children from the village nearby. The Depression, however, was making funding difficult. The last session, the Nature Guide School on Wheels, was a bus trip to New England with 25 graduate students majoring in elementary science. What an incalculable influence that study tour must have had on those young teachers visiting Niagara, Mohawk Valley, Bear Mountain, Monadnock, Mount Washington, Plymouth, and Cape Cod!

The years 1935 through 1937 saw Vinal on an itinerant team with other experts in the National Recreation Association. He visited 24 major cities in the eastern United States to stimulate, among other efforts, formation of field study courses and nature clubs. He was learning, however, that it takes more than a two-week session to train nature leaders for camps and other youth and community groups. He needed more time to help them grow.

So from 1938 to 1951, he was professor of nature recreation at the University of Massachusetts, Amherst. There he influenced countless students with whom he had much more than short-term contact. In fact, after graduation from the two-year or four-year courses, countless alumni kept contact with their beloved Cap'n Bill, either by returning to the Annual Nature Recreation Conferences at Amherst or by other visits and correspondence.

During his Amherst years, Vinal was not in an academic closet. No tenured doldrums for him! For six summers, 1941-1946, he led a lively outdoor life as naturalist for National Camp, also called Life Camps, and later Trail Blazer Camps, at Sussex, New Jersey, along with Dr. L. B. Sharp and other notables in resident outdoor education. There was great sharing there. Many of his university students were counselors along with those from New York and New Jersey State Teachers Colleges. Cap'n Bill reminisced, "If successful at living in the wilderness with eight New York City kids of various nationalities, one could be successful anywhere."

Dr. Vinal's support of decentralized camping extended beyond his efforts to promote small units of established camps as at Life Camps. For instance, he came to the aid of American Youth Hosteling, whose founders Monroe and Isabelle Smith he met at neighboring Northfield. In 1947 he sailed to Europe on a youth ship with 200 young people dedicated through world fellowship to help restore areas destroyed by World War II. He had a double mission: to write a manual of hosteling for the AYH and to make a survey of European national parks, forests, nature preserves, and trailside museums for the International Council of Museums.

Closer to home, from 1939 to 1951, Vinal collaborated with the Conservation Council of Massachusetts to provide a naturalist visiting service to resident camps in New England, staffed by some of his best students. Consultation and evening programs helped divert many a camp from a too-regimented program of blow-the-whistle athletics, opening the eyes of campers and camp administrators to the natural world around them. In that era many camps had so-called nature counselors who were misplaced city biology teachers in a "nature cabin" cutting up frogs to show the gonads to the kids. Vinal's conservation van helped counter that! There was more healthy excitement waiting outdoors—and with just as much sex.

Vinal students were encouraged to partake of field experience in a remarkable array of community situations from slums to mountaintops. Their reports back to fellow students (not just to professors) at the end of a summer or term away created continuing shared excitement for nature-related human service.

One of Cap'n Bill's fortes was stump scouting, wherein a person with curiosity (anybody who had not jelled prematurely) would approach a stump or other piece of wood and try to figure out its heredity and environmental influences from a close study of its growth rings and other grain characteristics. His own radiant personality did not pour information into them; rather it energized them to be seekers on their own. His own personal philosophy became available to them by example and not by dictation. His personal quest for ways to serve humanity opened many doors to them. He would point a path he had taken and then follow to support them so long as needed. One could never say of him, this "professor is one who stands between a student and his subject,"—thereby cutting off the light.

The measure of Vinal's bigness is not his own growth rings such as those hinted at in this chapter. The bigness of his contribution to resident outdoor education as well as to many other educational and recreational ventures is better measured by the contributions of the thousands whom he touched. The ripple effect often used to describe great people who make a big splash is not a good figure of speech to describe Vinal's influence. Rather he was a particular pebble whose radiating energies became higher and higher waves as his students went forth into the world for which he so ably prepared them, a world that needed them, a world where man and nature must be understood to be inseparable.

Acknowledgements

1. Autobiographical notes in *Nature Study,* Volume 28, Number 4, Winter 1974-1975. A special issue of 62 pages devoted entirely to Dr. Vinal by The American Nature Study Society.
2. Chequesset material graciously supplied by Doris Holmes, Librarian at the South Shore Natural Science Center, Norwell, Massachusetts 02061.

© Donald Rettew

Chapter 3

CONTRIBUTIONS OF LLOYD B. SHARP

FIFTY YEARS OF RESIDENT OUTDOOR EDUCATION: 1930-1980

by Thomas J. Rillo

Thomas J. Rillo, Ph.D.
Professor of Recreation and Outdoor Education
Indiana University

Dr. Thomas J. Rillo has been teaching at various levels for twenty-seven years. He spent seven years teaching in the public schools of New Jersey. His first college assignment was as assistant professor of education and coordinator of outdoor education at Montclair State College in New Jersey. During this time he was also associated with the New Jersey State School of Conservation. Dr. Rillo was associate professor of outdoor education, chairman of the Outdoor Education Division, and coordinator of the Outdoor Education Center, all at Southern Illinois University. He was professor of environmental education at Glassboro State College in New Jersey, and presently is a professor of recreation and outdoor education at Indiana University.

Much of his background can be attributed to his long association with the late Dr. Lloyd B. Sharp, noted authority in outdoor education. He has been active in outdoor education and environmental education for more than thirty years.

Dr. Rillo has been instrumental in the initiation of many public school outdoor education programs and has served as a consultant and master planner for numerous outdoor education programs and facilities. He is the author of numerous publications concerning outdoor education and environmental education and is a consulting editor for the *Journal of Environmental Education, Science Activities Magazine,* and *The Communicator—New York State Journal of Outdoor Education.*

Lloyd Burgess Sharp was born on March 22, 1895, in Carbondale, Kansas. As youngsters, his parents had moved with their parents by wagon from Whitehouse, N.J., to the small rural farming community located southeast of Topeka, Kansas. L. B. Sharp was greatly influenced by his early years on the farm. He did most of the chores of farm boys during this era. During his free time he would hunt, fish, trap, and in general reflect on his rural surroundings. He was quite proud of his farm background, and, in later years, would often reflect on these experiences as parallels to outdoor education.

One favorite story he would relate was about the creativity of a *Certain Kansas Lad*. This was the title of an autobiography which, unfortunately, he was never able to complete. It seems that one of Sharp's chores on the farm was to feed the livestock each day. He found it quite tedious to pull the hay down from the loft with a pitchfork and spread it about for each animal to eat. He had an idea to drill a hole in the handle of the pitchfork and string it on a wire which ran the entire length of the barn. This enabled him to retrieve the pitchfork without bending over, thereby conserving his energy. The procedure was working well until he tried to feed the farm mule. When he released the pitchfork to spread the hay for the mule, the pitchfork jerked up rapidly and then descended even faster, piercing the mule's ear just as the animal bent over to eat. The mule leaped back and violently kicked a hole through the wall of the stall, ran across the barnyard, and right through Mother Sharp's vegetable garden. Father Sharp, observing through the kitchen window, quietly, but firmly, suggested to L. B. that he return to the more traditional method of feeding the animals. L. B. Sharp often remarked in later years that his creativity was nipped in the budding stage and thereby caused him to become an educator rather than a famous inventor.

This story was an example of the many anecdotes from which he drew in order to put across a point or value position relative to outdoor education, and was a definite part of his colorful and dynamic personality. There is no doubt that this early farm experience gave him a sense of self-reliance and resourcefulness that was to be useful to him throughout his pioneering career in outdoor education.

His early schooling was in Carbondale where he attended a rural school. An occasion where he had to take over the fifth and sixth grade classes for the teacher influenced his decision to enter the field of education. As a twelfth grader he took over the class for an extended period of time while the teacher recovered from an illness. L. B. used to say that he had such a good time teaching, he hoped Miss Hartman would not come back too soon.

He later attended Kansas State Teachers College in Emporia, Kansas, where he excelled in football, track, and the academic program. His original intention was to enter the field of teaching and do some coaching of football and track. However, World War I was going on when he graduated from college in 1918 and he entered the Navy and served as an Ensign in the signal division. Upon his discharge from the Navy, L. B. Sharp did some part-time teaching, and then in 1924 matriculated at Columbia University. He received his master's degree in 1927 and his Ph.D. in 1929, thus becoming the first person to receive a doctorate in camping education.

While at Columbia University, L. B. Sharp had many classes with a group of faculty members known as "The New Educators." This group represented the experimental school of educational philosophy and its members were also known as pragmatists. John Dewey, a foremost pioneer in the area of progressive education, was the pragmatist who most influenced L. B. Sharp. William Heard Kilpatrick, Boyd Bode, and Elbert K. Fretwell were among the New Educators who influenced his thinking on how children and youth should learn.

On January 1, 1925, while L. B. Sharp was pursuing a master's degree, his career in camping and outdoor education began with an invitation to work with Life Camps. Life Camps had its beginning in the spring of 1887, under the sponsorship of the old *Life* magazine. At that time, and up to 1925, the name of the organization was Life's Fresh Air Fund. During this thirty-eight-year period, Life's Fresh Air Fund offered free vacations for children at two places known as Fresh Air Farms. This was part of a large movement, chiefly in New York City, known as Fresh Air Work. Many underprivileged children were taken to the two farms operated by Life's Fresh Air Fund, the girls to Branchville, Connecticut, and the boys to Pottersville, New Jersey. By 1924 the program had degenerated to deplorable standards of operation.

A prominent social service organization recommended that a survey be made of the Life Fresh Air Farms Program. Mrs. Edith Shatto King of the social service organization approached Columbia University asking for assistance in evaluating and reconstructing Life Fresh Air Farms. L. B. Sharp was chosen to make the study and recommendations, and he met with Mrs. King. He recalled in later years that he agreed to do the study only if the organization would change the name from Life Fresh Air Farms to Life Camps. L. B. Sharp said to Mrs. King, "I don't know how to farm fresh air, but I do know how to farm pigs, wheat, and corn." He was employed by Life Fresh Air Fund beginning January 1, 1925. What he discovered was horrendous.

The program was conducted in a highly militaristic manner. In regimented fashion, bugles blared, horns and whistles resounded. The program was highly structured, and the facilities were arranged in colinear array. The counselor-camper ratio was one to fifty. The campers had a separate menu which consisted of porridge, stew and soup cooked in one pot. The campers had only bowls and spoons with which to eat. Counselors had a different menu which was superior to that of the campers, and they ate in seperate facilities. Sharp wrote a fourteen point report and submitted it to the Life Fresh Air Fund Committee. One of his major recommendations was that they employ someone to reorganize the camping program.

In the spring of 1925, L. B. Sharp was named executive director of Life Camps. The first step he undertook was to employ new staff who could work with children and youth on a small group basis in the out-of-doors. The first counselor he employed was Sophia "Rya" Gelavitz, a Massachusetts schoolteacher, who was working at a Girl Scout Camp in Bear Mountain State Park in New York. On her own she was already working with girls in an innovative decentralized camping program.

It is here that we can begin to see the *first contribution* of L. B. Sharp to the field of camping and outdoor education. It was basically the transferral to a camp setting of what he had learned about teaching methodology and learning environments from the New Educators at Columbia University. Experimentation was begun in 1927 with the small group process, and the first small camp or outpost camp was established. The results in individual growth and development were so successful that the entire program was soon reorganized and conducted on a small group plan in both of the children's camps.

Sharp's Criteria for Change

In 1926 Sharp had presented a five point criteria of what he thought should occur if positive changes were to be made in the campers. *First*, the counselors should state their major aims or purposes concerning the campers and their program. This would provide an overall reference point to be constantly striven for and represented an upward reach which may be measured. *Second*, the counselors were to write specific objectives for each aim. These were mileposts along the way that should be measured. They represented the immediate goals that could be reached in an adequately conducted program. *Third*, the procedures for reaching the objectives should be clearly written by the counselors. *Fourth*, the objectives and procedures should be evalu-ated in terms of their functional applications both throughout and at the end of the camping program. *Fifth*, after reviewing the first four points, there must be an investigation as to what was learned and how this information would help future programs. For the first time Sharp required the counselors to set forth in writing what they anticipated would happen to their campers in such areas as health, food, sanitation, nature, conservation, and spiritual or religious values.

The five point criteria had to be applied by all camp staff members, not just counselors. Most of the procedures for their assignment were developed during pre-camp training conferences. At this time the first three points were considered for development. Each staff member developed a major aim along with the objectives and procedures which they anticipated reaching during the summer. This activity helped Sharp to identify where changes were to be made in the Life Camps program. It was the beginning of the small group approach known as decentralized camping. It also marked the beginning of a concerted effort to make education an integral part of the total camping program.

Changes in Camping Philosophy

Beginning in 1926, accurate records of both the boys' and girls' camps were kept. These were titled, *Annual Report of Boys' Life Camps* and *Annual Report of Girls' Life Camps*, and were bound separately for each year. No other writing about this program more clearly depicts the changes in camping philosophy than these reports of Life Camps submitted each year. Very early in these reports the philosophy embraced by L. B. Sharp is evident. One can visualize when the departmentalized "special-taught" activities type of program was completely broken up and campers were put on their own in order to facilitate the elements of adventure, exploration and discovery. The reports show the opportunities that were extended to campers to increase their skills in outdoor living. They were given a chance to build their own shelters wherever feasible, to plan their own programs, to cook most of their own meals, to plan and care for gardens, to go on extensive one, two, or three day trips exploring the countryside, and to learn how to live and work with others in small groups.

As a result of this adventurous pioneering type of camping, many new shelters were designed and utilized. The Life Camps used hogans, round-to's, tepees, covered wagons, covered sleds, tree houses, and a variety of other innovative shelters.

To L. B. Sharp, camping was "loving to live in the

woods and open spaces" and he believed that a camp program should be reflective of a program for life. He stipulated that a good camp program should be developed around the need for food, shelter, self occupation, group relationships, and spiritual uplift. He saw these to be inherent in a good program of daily living, and felt that a good camp should approximate these five points. Decentralized camping was, perhaps, his *second major contribution* to outdoor education. L. B. Sharp could be viewed as the "Father of Decentralized Camping," especially as an organized, full scale program.

In an article written for *Camping Magazine* in 1940, Sharp focused on the advantages of decentralized camping:

> . . . Campers and counselors live in small groups—six to eight campers and two counselors with them. They have their own camp all to themselves. They plan most of their own meals, secure provisions from the camp store and keep their own food costs.(1)

An increasing number of visitors came each year to study this unique program. Educators began to see its possibilities in the field of education.

Early in his association with Life Camps, L. B. Sharp recognized the educational values of a well-planned and administered camp program. His doctoral dissertation emphasized this recognition when he stated:

> Camping provides opportunities for activities which are in themselves real life situations, as the campers are largely dependent upon their own efforts for their personal care and safety, and the care and use of equipment.(2)

Again in the same dissertation he stipulated that:

> By the very nature of the situation, the campers are placed more upon their own resources because the sources of aid are limited. They have opportunities for choosing projects from among those which naturally present themselves in a camp situation, and are free to work them out to a completion, according to their own design.(3)

In his dissertation written in 1929, L. B. Sharp coined the term "Camping Education." This represents a *third major contribution* of L. B. Sharp to outdoor education, namely that of focusing on the educational benefits of camping for a variety of institutions, including the school system of a community. Hence the term "Father of Camping Education" can honestly be attributed to him.

L. B. Sharp continued his research and study of the effects of camping on education throughout the 1930s. In an article written in March, 1935, for *Camping Magazine* he stated that school camping up to that time had been conducted mostly during the summer months:

> It is indeed unfortunate for our children that so many excellent educational facilities lie idle during the large part of the year—an educational waste. Camping is beneficial in the winter as in summer and the public school camp should be open all year.(4)

Here we can see L. B. Sharp's emphasis on public school camping begin to appear in the literature. Thus the title, "Father of Public School Camping," can be attributed to Sharp. This represents his *fourth major contribution* to outdoor education, namely that of alerting school authorities on a national level to the values of public school camping during the regular academic year.

From 1936 to 1940, educators increasingly began to consider camping as a part of the school curriculum. Life Camps and L. B. Sharp were called upon to explain to educational groups the program of Life Camps, its effect on children, its methods, and accomplishments. *Youth in Camps*, a 16 millimeter motion picture film, depicting the general type of camping in the United States, and especially the Life Camps program, was completed in 1938. Appearing in this film, John Dewey made the following statement:

> The average American child seldom comes in direct contact with nature. In school he learns a few dates from books, to press a button, to step on an accelerator; but he is in danger of losing contact with primitive realities—with the world, with the space about us, with fields and with the problems of getting shelter and obtaining food that have always conditioned human life and that still do.(5)

A four-year project was carried out in cooperation with the New York City schools from 1939 through 1942. Mrs. Johana Lindlof, then a member of the City Board of Education, created the Johana Lindlof Camp Fund to help finance the project. The results of the experiment were published in pamphlet form and entitled *Adventuring in Camping Education*.

Development of Leadership Training

By 1940, L. B. Sharp realized that there was a real need to give leadership to this movement and direction at all levels of education, and also to establish a center for the training of advanced leadership. Life Camps by now were operating at three locations. The younger boys went to Camp Raritan located in Pottersville, New Jersey, and the older boys went to Camp Pole Bridge in Milford, Pennsylvania. The girls' camp was relocated in Sussex, New Jersey, where a beautiful facility was completed in 1939. This site, located near Lake Mashipacong, above High Point State Park, was acquired through the generosity of Doris Duke, the tobacco heiress. This site was also selected for the location of National Camp which was completed by 1940. Actual work began on the building program on April 15, 1940, and on July 9 of the same year National Camp opened with twenty-one adults from seventeen states and Canada.

New York University began its cooperation with National Camp during that first year. Through New York University, six semester hours of graduate credit were available to the participants in the summer institutes and could be applied toward graduate degrees. The institute programs conducted during June at National Camp were begun with the State Teachers Colleges of New Jersey in 1941. New York State Teachers Colleges joined the institute programs in 1942. In these ten-day institutes, thousands of college students and faculty were introduced to the idea and movement known as public school camping. As a result, many of these colleges developed their own facilities and programs.

Two significant experiments in school camping were conducted at National Camp during June of 1944, 1945, and 1946. The purpose of these experiments was to demonstrate how camping education could be correlated with the school curriculum. The first project in 1944 was with the Lanning Demonstration School of Trenton State Teachers College. The principal, George Donaldson, the teachers, and the thirty-two fifth and sixth grade children came to National Camp for a ten-day school camping program. This project was repeated in June, 1945. Many other school camping programs emanated from this experiment. The second school camp project, in 1946, was conducted in cooperation with the Demonstration High School of Montclair State Teachers College. This lent further impetus to the feasibility of school camping at the junior high school level.

National Camp and its program represents L. B. Sharp's *fifth major contribution* to outdoor education, namely that of perpetuating the concept of school camping through leadership training. Sharp was assisted at National Camp by a very professional and competent staff. The staff included such outstanding outdoor educators as William (Cap'n Bill) Gould Vinal, William (Moosewood Bill) Harlow, E. DeAlton Partridge, Reynold Carlson, and Phillip Walker. Lois Goodrich and Sophia "Rya" Gelavitz were two Life Camp staff members who assisted greatly in the National Camp Institute Program. Each student attending National Camp was required to work on a specific problem related to implementing outdoor education in their own communities. These problems were published and bound each year and were called *National Camp Problems*.

It was through National Camp and its program that L. B. Sharp was able to influence many potential outdoor education leaders from many different states. Through them he was able to project his philosophy of outdoor education throughout the country. Somewhere between 1944 and 1946, Sharp began to use the term outdoor education synonymously with public school camping. Because of National Camp and its resultant program, the title "Father of Outdoor Education" can quite honestly be bestowed upon L. B. Sharp. It is just a matter of simple chronological adjustment, for he was the first nationally recognized leader in the area of outdoor education.

The Outdoor Education Method

A *sixth major contribution* which L. B. Sharp made to outdoor education is exemplified in a simplistic, but logical, thesis. When he first coined the thesis is difficult to pinpoint, but he formally presented this thesis in an article which he wrote in 1943. He stated:

> That which ought and can best be taught inside the schoolrooms should there be taught, and that which can best be learned through experience dealing directly with native materials and life situations outside the school should there be learned.(6)

This, perhaps, represents the biggest contribution L. B. Sharp made to the philosophy of outdoor education. He merely asked for the application of this thesis to the on-going curriculum of the school. That which could most effectively and efficiently be learned in the out-of-doors constituted the outdoor education program. This thesis has been quoted more often over the years than anything else Sharp wrote. It appeared in hundreds of outdoor education curriculum guides and manuals, and has withstood the test of time, for it is still being quoted today.

It was also here that L. B. Sharp defined outdoor education as a method or climate for learning. To him it was not a subject, nor was it a department. It was merely an interdisciplinary approach to more effective and efficient learning. This definition represents his *seventh major contribution* to outdoor education. It projected the theory that no two outdoor education programs ever need be alike, for the needs of individuals or groups from diverse educational programs and geographical areas would be different. Sharp held no argument with a program that included outdoor manipulative skills if there was a real need for their inclusion in the program.

In the summer of 1946, many outstanding education leaders convened at National Camp. Under the general chairmanship of Dr. Walter D. Cocking, the committee was charged with the task of discussing the basic issues in camping and outdoor education and coming up with recommendations. These issues were:

1. What is the place of outdoor education in American education?
2. How can camping and outdoor education be integrated into higher education?
3. How can public support for camping and outdoor education be developed so it can be extended to more American youth?

In June, 1947, National Camp became the setting for a significant pioneer experiment in school camping and outdoor education. This experiment was conducted by the staff of Life Camps in cooperation with the New York City Board of Education. Two classrooms of fifth and seventh grade students from two New York City schools spent three weeks at Life Camps during school time. There were sixty-four students selected on a matched-pair basis. Those who went to camp did not take their school books, nor did they have formal class instruction. An elaborate testing program was set up under the supervision of Dr. J. Wayne Wrightstone, City Schools psychologist. The experimental or camping group was checked against the control groups which stayed in school and studied in the traditional manner. The results demonstrated that in nearly all the tests, the camp group equaled or bettered the ones who stayed in school. In addition, there were educational gains in social living, cooperation, understanding among different religions and racial groups not possible in the traditional school environment.

The experiment and results were published in book form entitled *Extending Education Through Camping*.(8) A sound motion picture film was produced about the experiment entitled *School Time in Camp*.(9)

The color film was widely circulated. This experiment represents L. B. Sharp's *eighth major contribution* to outdoor education. It ranks as one of the greatest contributions he made, for it established the fact that outdoor education was academically sound and could be an extension of the regular curricular program. By today's research standards, the experiment could be dissected with some negative connotations. However, for its day it was highly significant. To this writer's knowledge, it has never been replicated.

The end of World War II heralded a greater challenge to the American educational system than ever before. Sharp was quick to note that if the schools were to meet the needs of American society, then those schools would have to change their traditional methods. He saw this and pointed out:

Our American schools today are faced with the tremendous task of improving the quality of our citizenship. Emphasis needs to be placed increasingly upon basic experiences and understanding of food, shelter, care of self, work, the practice of conservation, development of resourcefulness and self-reliance, healthful living, racial and religious understanding, individual and group cooperation, and a wholesome respect for and love of country. The trend is toward more realism—realism meaning more learning through direct experience. Outdoor education is all of that learning which can best go on through direct experience outside the classroom. The out-of-doors begins immediately outside the classroom and continues in an ever widening circle, the finest classroom ever devised.(10)

At this time, L. B. Sharp became very much interested in the short-term approach to outdoor education or school site and community resource use. Although the idea had been experimented with and written about earlier by others such as William G. Vinal and E. Laurence Palmer of Cornell University, Sharp pioneered the need for school site outdoor education. In an article written for the *School Executive* publication, Sharp emphasized his interest in short-term outdoor education:

The first step out of the school building takes you far enough to find some of the things in nature that are pictured and described in the school books. First, there is the earth, then even in the poorest neighborhoods, some plant growth, a great deal of weather, and always some animal or insect life. Beyond the school yard lies the community, a fit subject for study, surely government, public health, safety, law and order, business, society, industry—all these should be seen firsthand if any useful knowledge of them is to be gathered. And out beyond the community, is the woods and open spaces. This is the outermost circle in which outdoor education operates, and it has a good many values of its own.(11)

One might regard this emphasis as L. B. Sharp's *ninth major contribution* to outdoor education, namely that of focusing attention on the need to begin outdoor education just beyond the classroom.

Seeing the need to provide information and services to various organizations and individuals involved in outdoor education, Sharp founded the Outdoor Education Association, Inc., in 1951. L. B. Sharp functioned as executive director of the association and also served as consultant and master planner for camps and outdoor education centers. He also contributed greatly to the development of church camping during this period. In 1951, Life and Time, Inc., discontinued its support of Life Camps and of National Camp. Sharp relocated National Camp to the Camp Pole Bridge site in Milford, Pennsylvania, and continued the National Camp Institutes, concentrating on church camp leaders. For ten years church camp personnel came to National Camp to study decentralized camping and Christian outdoor education.

© Donald Rettew

Here we can see both the *tenth* and *eleventh major contributions* which L. B. Sharp extended to outdoor education. The *tenth contribution* was represented by the fact that he established the first national organization devoted to outdoor education. This was an extremely timely organization which accomplished a great deal in organizing outdoor educators into a unified body. The *eleventh major contribution* is represented by his active involvement with church camping and Christian outdoor education. While not the first to coin the term, Sharp certainly helped to make Christian outdoor education an accepted aspect of church camping programs.

In 1960, Southern Illinois University invited L. B. Sharp to relocate the national headquarters of the Outdoor Education Association to the campus. He was also given professorial rank and charged with the development of an outdoor education center for the thirty-one southernmost counties of Illinois. While at Southern Illinois University, L. B. Sharp began to experiment with a new concept he had earlier introduced at National Camp concerned with the use of mobile trailers. These small trailers could be used either on the school site or at a location to which the students would travel and utilize the trailer as a base for outdoor learning.

The trailer concept was originally developed for trailer travel camping. This began in 1955 with the campers in residence at National Camp. The trailer was designed so that it could be constructed by a camp maintenance staff or in a school industrial arts shop. It was built of exterior plywood with a metal frame and was divided into three basic sections. The center section was used for carrying equipment such as tents, sleeping bags, etc. One side was a fully equipped camping kitchen. The other side included a library and outdoor instructional equipment such as hand lenses, magnetic compasses, microscopes, binoculars, dip nets, etc.

At Southern Illinois University, Sharp utilized the trailer both on the school site and on location at the outdoor education center. In support of this concept, Sharp stated:

. . . education should be on wheels, it must roll and it must move. We have been entirely too stationary. I would hope that there would be more mobility.(12)

It was during this time that he coined a nomenclature entitled "*Land for Learning.*" To Sharp the program always determined the facilities. Land for Learning was a designated natural area devoted to outdoor education. The trailers, instead of permanent facilities, were used on the land because they had a minimum amount of environmental impact. This represents his *twelfth major contribution*. It illustrated that outdoor education did not have to have elaborate facilities and that one should invest in land rather than facilities at the outset of any program. There should be mobility and flexibility to outdoor education programs, and they could be conducted wherever there was open space to do so. He felt that outdoor education should be more than just a one-week experience in the life of the school child. He stressed the extension of the program down to the kindergarten level as well as upward. He felt that there was a great deal of potential leadership in the upper grades of the secondary school and that they should be utilized in the program.

During the years the Outdoor Education Association functioned, L. B. Sharp was often asked to conduct surveys for church camps, outdoor education centers, and other agency camps. It was while he was in the field conducting such a survey for a church camp near Mayo, Florida, that he died on December 4, 1963.

He had been one of the most colorful and dynamic personalities in the field of camping and outdoor education. He had exhibited a singleness of purpose and was completely dedicated to the values of outdoor living and learning for American youth. He was "a voice in the wilderness" when he started his professional career, and he often stood alone in his convictions. Very often these same strong convictions placed him in conflict with others. It has been said that when one stands on principles it can be a very lonely place. There were times when loneliness was a constant companion for L. B. Sharp. In the beginning it was Sharp who was the focal point of the movement; however, his followers have continued his work and philosophy even though modern times have necessitated some modifications.

Larry Conrad delivered an address at the dedication of the L. B. Sharp Memorial Library at the New Jersey State School of Conservation entitled, "A Tribute to Dr. L. B. Sharp." His words were most fitting in describing the character and philosophy of L. B. Sharp. This close friend, a professor emeritus of English from Montclair State College, New Jersey, delivered these most appropriate words:

> The upshot of all L. B. Sharp's work could be a better adjustment to the environment and atmosphere of learning, or perhaps simply more attention to that element, wherever the classes are conducted. For he only insisted that everything in the educational process should be carried out in its own optimum sphere. Any such adjustments could bring about many improvements in indoor learning. But his work and wisdom surely call for a

more frequent and widespread journeying forth from the classroom into the world—which is where all the material is to be found, about which we are undertaking to study.(13))

L. B. Sharp was not one to remain stagnant and unmoving and he continued to grow and change with the times. He was always willing to go beyond the status quo. There is no doubt that he would have embraced the concept of environmental education with the same zeal and enthusiasm he had for camping education. Perhaps the ultimate contribution that he made to outdoor education was his willingness to put his career and his life, as it turned out, into one vital and potent concept.

Selected References

1. Sharp, L. B., "Giving Camping Back to the Campers," *Camping Magazine,* Vol. XII, No. 3, March, 1940, p. 7.
2. Sharp, L. B. *Education and the Summer Camp—An Experiment* New York: Teachers College, Columbia University, 1930, p. 41.
3. Ibid.
4. Sharp, L. B., "The Public School Camp," *Camping Magazine*, Vol. VII, No. 3, March, 1935, p. 28.
5. *Youth in Camps*, Motion picture sponsored by Life-Time, Inc., 1938.
6. Sharp, L. B., "Outside the Classroom," *The Educational Forum*, Vol. VII, No. 4, May, 1943, pp. 363-364.
7. Partridge, E. DeAlton, Editor, "Basic Issues in Camping and Outdoor Education," *Extending Education*, Vol. III, No. 3 November, 1946, pp. 1-8.
8. *Extending Education Through Camping*. New York: Life Camps, Inc., 1948, pp. 9-130.
9. *School Time in Camp*, Motion Picture Film produced by Life Camps, Inc., and the March of Time, 1948.
10. Sharp, L. B., "Outdoor and Camping Education," *Extending Education*, Vol. IV, No. 1, May, 1949, p. 1.
11. Sharp, L. B., "What is Outdoor Education?" *The School Executive*, Vol. 15, No. 8, August 1952, p. 19.
12. Sharp, L. B., "Outdoor Education is Off the Pad" *Extending Education*, Vol. VI, No. 1, September, 1961, p. 4.
13. Conrad, Lawrence H., "A Tribute to Dr. L. B. Sharp," spoken at the dedication of the L. B. Sharp Memorial Library at the New Jersey State School of Conservation, May 6, 1964.

Roger B. Hill

Chapter 4

CONTRIBUTIONS OF JULIAN W. SMITH

FIFTY YEARS OF RESIDENT OUTDOOR EDUCATION: 1930-1980

by Reynold E. Carlson

Reynold E. Carlson, Dr.H.

Professor Emeritus
Department of Recreation
    and Park Administration
Indiana University

Outdoor education has been a major interest of Reynold E. Carlson throughout most of his professional life. After graduating from the University of California, he served as a YMCA director, teacher, elementary school principal, and Yosemite Park ranger-naturalist. Then for eleven years he directed the nature and outdoor recreation services of the National Recreation Association and conducted leadership courses in many cities throughout the United States.

Carlson served as a professor in the Department of Recreation and Park Administration at Indiana University from 1947 to 1972, serving as department chairman for four years. His teaching was largely related to outdoor education and outdoor recreation. During this period he was, to a great extent, responsible for developing the Bradford Woods Outdoor Education and Camping Center, where for eighteen summers he conducted a field course in outdoor education.

Since retiring from Indiana University in 1973, Carlson has taught a number of short courses in colleges and universities, conducted and participated in workshops, served as a consultant and speaker, and done a considerable amount of writing. He is a member of the Advisory Committee on Lands, Forests, and Wildlife of the Indiana Department of Natural Resources and a member of the Ohio River Basin Commission Citizen's Advisory Committee.

Carlson has served as president of the American Camping Association and as chairman of a number of committees related to camping and outdoor education. He was prominent among those who were instrumental in bringing to Bradford Woods the Interpretive Naturalists Workshops from which developed the Association of Interpretive Naturalists. In 1962 he received the Lieber Award for outstanding teaching at Indiana University. Springfield College awarded him the honorary Doctor of Humanics degree in 1967. He has received numerous other awards, including Fellow Award from the Association of Interpretive Naturalists, Taft Campus Award for Outstanding Contributions to Outdoor Education, Distinguished Service Awards from the National Park and Recreation Association and the American Camping Association.

Carlson's writings include well over a hundred articles, booklets, studies, and special publications dealing with outdoor education, camping, and outdoor recreation. He is co-author of the following textbooks: Smith, Donaldson, Carlson, and Masters, *Outdoor Education*; Hanson and Carlson, *Organizations for Children and Youth*; and Carlson, MacLean, Deppe, and Peterson, *Recreation and Leisure—The Changing Scene*.

Although the roots of outdoor education cannot be precisely traced and many men and women have contributed to the growth of the movement, Julian Warner Smith stands out as one of the few who, with persistent devotion, guided the movement and influenced its character with his philosophy, principles, and active leadership.

Julian Smith was born July 18, 1901, at Leslie, Michigan, about twenty miles south of Lansing.(1) He grew up on a small farm, attended Woodland High School and Hastings High School; then went on to graduate from the Barry County Normal in 1920. After teaching for two years in Woodland, he went to Western Michigan University, where he completed work for a life certificate in 1923. He served as principal, teacher, and coach at the Woodland Township Consolidated School until 1927 and then resumed his education, receiving a Bachelor of Arts degree from the University of Michigan in 1928. He then became principal of Lakeview High School at Battle Creek, where he stayed for fourteen years. Meanwhile, in 1936, he earned his Master of Arts degree from the University of Michigan.

In Battle Creek he began a cooperative program with the W. K. Kellogg Foundation and Hugh B. Masters, its educational director, that resulted in the first year-round school camping program of the United States. This program was initiated at the Foundation's Clear Lake Camp in 1940.

During World War II (1942-1945), Smith served as the director of interscholastic athletics for the state of Michigan. After the war he became Assistant Superintendent of Public Instruction in charge of Health, Physical Education, and Recreation. The Michigan program was soon expanded to include school camping and outdoor education. In 1946, with funds from the Kellogg Foundation, the Outdoor Education State Project was launched, with Smith as assistant supervisor. By the time the project terminated in 1953, Michigan had become the national leader in outdoor education. Julian's broad interests were evident during this period through his development of a work-learn camp for high school dropouts and the Michigan Interagency Council on Recreation. His programs always functioned in close cooperation with the Michigan State Conservation Department.

In 1953 Julian Smith was appointed Associate Professor of Education at Michigan State University; he became a professor in 1964 and professor emeritus in 1972. His intense interest in the growing outdoor education field led to the establishment in 1955 of the Outdoor Education Project of the American Association for Health, Physical Education and Recreation (now the American Alliance for Health, Physical Education and Recreation) in cooperation with various sporting goods businesses and industries. He served as director of this project until his death on June 23, 1975.

The establishment of the Council on Outdoor Education of the AAHPER in 1964 was one of the high points of Smith's career. He served part of the time as liaison of the council.

The honors that Julian Smith received during his lifetime are too numerous to list here. A few of them were the honorary doctorate of education from Eastern Michigan University in 1955, and the Hedley S. Dimock award from the American Camping Association in 1970. He received the Luther H. Gulick Award, the highest honor bestowed by AAHPER, in 1972, in recognition of his leadership in "promoting the expansion of outdoor education as an integral and significantly contributing aspect of American education."

The Outdoor Education Project

The last twenty years of Dr. Smith's life were devoted primarily to the Outdoor Education Project of the AAHPER. During this time his greatest contributions to outdoor education were made. In his early years his efforts were directed toward promoting school camping and encouraging schools to use the outdoors for educational purposes. In these later years he broadened his concept, as he saw it, to develop the various outdoor-related skills as well. He saw the Outdoor Education Project as a large umbrella under which could be included all aspects of learning, understanding, and appreciating the outdoors, and the skills related to its use. He considered outdoor education a means of life enrichment as well as environmental conservation. In his words, the project was "the only national educational effort devoted solely to outdoor education in its broadest aspects."(2)

Michigan State University was generous in making his services available on a national basis. Thus, in 1955, a program began that was to take him back and forth across the nation, conducting workshops, meeting with school officials, giving talks, attending conferences, working with college and university leaders, and conferring with individuals and groups representing a wide variety of related organizations. The project was financed in part by several sporting goods interests whose concern lay not only in sales, but also in the wise use and enjoyment of the environment.

The Outdoor Education Project involved three major thrusts: teacher and leadership preparation, interpretation, and publications. Of these, the greatest emphasis was placed upon teacher and leadership preparation.

The movement could progress only as teachers, administrators, and leaders from camping, recreation, and conservation fields could be prepared for service.

More than 400 state and regional workshops and clinics with over 35,000 participants were conducted in 46 states between 1955 and 1975 under the auspices of the Outdoor Education Project.(3) These were intended to improve teaching skills as well as to develop a philosophy of outdoor use and understanding. The state and regional meetings led to local clinics and workshops that carried the message to the grass roots. How many individuals were reached directly or indirectly by this program is hard to determine, but the measure of their effectiveness lies in the expansion of programs both in outdoor skills and in outdoor learning.

Another emphasis of the Outdoor Education Project was the encouragement of colleges and universities to expand outdoor education and outdoor recreation programs. By 1970, 425 graduate credit workshops were being conducted by colleges and universities with an estimated 17,500 teachers participating.

Another significant service during these years was the conducting of Summer Graduate Outdoor Education Workshops, sponsored by the Outdoor Education Project and Michigan State University. These workshops, held at Gull Lake and Kellogg Center in Michigan from 1955 to 1975, brought together 1,050 graduate students from thirty-five states and four Canadian provinces.

These programs provided greater depth than was possible in the shorter workshops presented throughout the country.

The second thrust of the Project, that of interpretation, included conducting five National Conferences on Outdoor Education, held at four-year intervals. The 1958 and 1966 conferences were held in Washington, D.C.; the 1962 and 1970 conferences at the Gull Lake Biological Station in Michigan; and the 1974 conference near Estes Park, Colorado. A sixth conference in 1972 was an international conference in Dorset, Ontario, at which Canada, the United States, and other countries were represented. These conferences brought together outdoor education leaders from a variety of education, recreational, and camping areas.

The third thrust of the project was the preparation and distribution of numerous articles, books, booklets, instructional materials, newsletters, and films. These were distributed largely through the American Alliance for Health, Physical Education and Recreation and were designed to assist teachers and leaders in the classroom and in the practical aspects of outdoor recreation instruction. Many articles appeared in the *Journal of Health, Physical Education and Recreation*.

Smith never paused in his efforts to inaugurate, improve, and expand interest in outdoor education. His personal contacts with administrators and instructors, especially in Departments of Health, Physical

© Phiz Mezey

Education and Recreation, with state directors of physical education, as well as with leaders in voluntary and public recreation agencies were just as fruitful as his formal writings, conferences, and workshops.

These years witnessed a tremendous growth in school outdoor programs. A survey by the Outdoor Education Project throughout the United States showed many gains in the number of outdoor education programs. For example, schools and colleges with outdoor skills programs expanded from 12 percent in 1955 to 50 percent in 1970; and those with resident outdoor education programs whose curriculum included spending one school week in camp settings grew from 300 districts in 1955 to 3,500 in 1975.(4) Although this expansion may be attributed to numerous factors, including the increased national concern for conservation, the interest of science teachers in direct experiences for students, and the general recognition by educators of the importance of environmental understanding, it must be recognized that the Outdoor Education Project played a large role in encouraging and directing this growth.

One of the crowning achievements of the project was the establishment of the Council on Outdoor Education of the AAHPER in 1964. This brought together into one organization representatives from many fields but particularly education, conservation, and recreation. Julian Smith served as liaison for the Council.

Dr. Smith was the originator of the Outdoor Education Project idea and the driving force behind its operations. He barnstormed America tirelessly from one end to the other in the interests of outdoor education. He gave the last twenty years of his life wholeheartedly to the project, while also teaching a limited number of classes at Michigan State University.

Education *in* and *for* the Outdoors

Dr. Smith's writings and talks amply revealed his philosophy of education *in* and *for* the outdoors. He felt strongly that many of modern society's problems sprang from the setting in which most of us live. He listed the causes of these problems as deterioration of the natural environment, urbanization, the frenzied tempo of modern living, mechanization, automation and computerization, sedentary living, abstractions, and materialism. In outdoor education he saw an antidote as well as a solution for the problems of society.

For the individual, he spoke of the need for creative living and the opportunities offered by increased leisure. He urged participation in art, drama, music, literature, and a host of outdoor pursuits, many with lifetime value. Because of his professional position, most of his

emphasis was upon the education of children and youth and their preparation for maturity. Particularly in his later years, however, he voiced the needs of older people and the responsibility of schools and recreation agencies to develop special programs for them.

In order to accomplish the goals of outdoor education, Dr. Smith embarked on a nationwide educational program for teachers and other leaders. The Outdoor Education Project placed emphasis on in-service education through workshops, clinics, and the inclusion of outdoor education in the curriculums of colleges and universities. Dr. Smith also promoted leadership education for diverse allied groups—workers in camping, recreation, conservation education, natural resources, and in fact all who dealt directly or indirectly with the outdoors. His program was intended not only for direct leaders, but also for administrators and policy formulators who were in the positions to implement the programs.

Smith saw "outdoor education" as encompassing the whole gamut of outdoor interests and felt that the different public and private associations might come together with the common bond of using, understanding, and appreciating the outdoors.

We cannot be sure when, where, and by whom the term "outdoor education" was first used. We do know that Dr. L. B. Sharp shifted from using the term "school camping" to using "outdoor education." The broadest interpretation of the term seems to have originated with Julian Smith. He wrote:

Outdoor education means learning *in* and *for* the outdoors. It is a means of curriculum extension and enrichment through outdoor experiences. It is not a separate discipline with prescribed objectives, like science and mathematics; it is simply a learning climate offering opportunities for direct laboratory experiences in identifying and resolving real-life problems, for acquiring skills with which to enjoy a lifetime of creative living, for building concepts and developing concern about man and his natural environment, and for getting us back in touch with those aspects of living where our roots were once firm and deep.(5)

Education *in* the Outdoors

In early use, the term, "outdoor education" referred primarily to the use of the outdoor environment for education, whether in school camp, school gardens, forests, or elsewhere on field trips. Emphasis was on natural science, although social studies, language arts, and physical education were also included. The concept broadened, as indicated in Dr. Smith's definition, through emphasis on education *in* the outdoors and *for* the outdoors. "*In* the outdoors" implied enriching the school curriculum by getting acquainted with the natural environment in all its aspects. The term also applied to the interpretive programs of conservation and recreation agencies and parks and to the outdoor services of youth agencies and organized camps. Its main thrust was toward the understanding, appreciation, and wise use of the outdoors in accord with biological principles essential to environmental protection.

The development of the Clear Lake Camp and his work with the Michigan State Department of Education in expanding school camping and promoting conservation enabled Dr. Smith to pursue this emphasis.

Education *for* the Outdoors

Although not in any way diminishing his concern for knowledge and understanding, Dr. Smith stressed the development of outdoor skills. "The outdoor sports," he wrote, "are not only compatible with the appreciation arts related to the outdoors, they are complementary and interrelated."(6) The skills he promoted included shooting and hunting, casting and angling, boating and water sports, archery, winter sports, hiking, bicycling, survival skills, use of map and compass, mountain climbing, woodsmanship, and many others. It was his conviction that the outdoorsman who had a stake in natural resources "must bear the awesome responsibility of maintaining an environment that has helped to make this nation great."(7) For this reason the education of the outdoor user was most important.

It was in this area of education for skills that Dr. Smith made one of his greatest contributions, which he promoted primarily as director of the Outdoor Education Project of the AAHPER.

His belief in the importance of education for leisure is expressed in these words: "American democracy, with the advantages of abundant resources, a system of free education, and highly developed industrialization has brought the golden age in this regard within reach, but—alas—many people lack the skills and appreciations to enter into the richer life which could be theirs. This may well be the great modern paradox because a society which has freed so many from long hours of toil has done little to prepare them for abundant life."(8) He looked to the community school as part of the answer to the need for education for leisure. He believed that it should be a center not only for children but for all ages

and should include education for leisure as a means of life enrichment. Not only did he promote the community school, but also, in his desire to find areas of cooperation among other organizations, he took part in national and state meetings of recreation organizations. Organized camping was another area of his concern. In the early days of the Clear Lake experiment, the program was known as School Camping and Conservation. He maintained a close relationship with the American Camping Association and participated in many of its workshops and conferences.

Julian Smith—the Man

Julian Smith was a life-long resident of southern Michigan, where he was born, reared, and educated. Here he married, raised a family, and built his career; and here he died. Yet from this small geographic area, through his tireless travels, teachings, writings, conferences, and personal contacts, his influence spread throughout the United States and Canada.

It would be difficult to find a man more dedicated. His academic life, his special services, and even his leisure were devoted to the promotion of outdoor education; and his hours were long.

Because the Outdoor Education Project was partially financed by sporting goods companies that were interested in encouraging outdoor skills, some people feared that Julian had sold out his interest in school outdoor education to commercial interests. The story is current that when it was suggested to him that he was using "tainted money" he replied with his usual good humor, "The only thing tainted about this money is that there 'tain't enough of it."

Those who really knew Smith recognized that throughout his life he remained consistent in his convictions. It must be remembered that his interest in physical education dated back to his earliest teaching days. It was logical that the Outdoor Education Project should be directed toward outdoor skills, since the project was sponsored by the American Alliance for Health, Physical Education and Recreation. At no time did he ever allow commercial concerns to influence his programs, nor did he abandon his belief in the importance of understanding and appreciating the natural environment. He continued to promote school environmental camps and centers and to encourage the expansion and improvement of environmental programs of public and voluntary agencies.

Julian Smith was a gentle man. Though strong in his convictions, he was always willing to listen to differing points of view and to give credit to others rather than to

expound upon his own achievements. In his quiet, unassuming manner, he was able to enlist cooperation and organize programs so as to achieve his desired goal. Though he was not an orator, he spoke with a ring of sincerity that captivated and inspired his audiences. He offered friendliness, and it was warmly returned.

Smith's love of nature and his love of God and humanity were as one. In a letter to a friend he wrote: "There is so much beauty in life if one could only be in the situation to find it and deeply feel and sense it all. The beauty really lies within the heart and the outward things only bring out those appreciations and love that are already there." In another letter, speaking of sunrise and sunset, he wrote, "Both are eternal and everlasting—a symbol of the love of God and His ordered universe."(9)

After his death, loving tributes to him revealed not only his own sensitivity toward the natural world but also his ability to awaken in others an awareness of its beauty.

Selected References

1. Much of the biographical data is gleaned from the doctoral dissertation by Lloyd David Williams, *Julian Warner Smith: His Life, Professional Career, and Contributions to Outdoor Education*, East Texas State University, 1976.
2. Julian W. Smith, "AAHPER Outdoor Education Project 1955-1970, A Review and Forward Look," *Journal of Health, Physical Education and Recreation*, February, 1970, p. 44.
3. Julian W. Smith, *The Outdoor Education Project, 1955-1975.* Mimeographed, Spring, 1975.
4. Ibid.
5. Julian W. Smith, Reynold Edgar Carlson, George W. Donaldson, and Hugh B. Masters, *Outdoor Education, Second Edition* Englewood Cliffs, New Jersey: Prentice Hall, Inc., 1972, p. 20.
6. Ibid., p. 147.
7. Ibid. p. 169.
8. Julian W. Smith, "My Philosophy of Recreation," *Recreation,* January, 1962, p. 7.
9. Excerpts from Julian Smith's correspondence with his friends.

Acknowledgments

I wish to give my greatest thanks to Charles A. Blackman, Assistant to the Dean for Continuing Education at Michigan State University, and to Norma Linn, Julian's secretary, for sending me considerable information, most of it unpublished, regarding Julian's life and work.

Editor's Note: Reynold Carlson first met Julian Smith when his career and reputation was confined largely to Michigan. Over the years they participated together in many conferences and workshops, cooperated in writing, and held many long conversations. As the years passed, Dr. Carlson was gratified to see the ideas and influence of Dr. Smith spread and grow across the nation.

Northern Illinois University

Chapter 5

IMPACT ON CAMPING EDUCATION

FIFTY YEARS OF RESIDENT OUTDOOR EDUCATION: 1930-1980

by Phyllis M. Ford

Phyllis M. Ford, Re.D.
Professor of Recreation and Park Management
University of Oregon

Phyllis Ford completed her B.S. degree under Dr. William G. "Cap'n Bill" Vinal at the University of Massachusetts, and her doctorate under Professor Reynold Carlson at Indiana University. These educational experiences helped to solidify an early interest in learning in and about the out-of-doors, and her professional career has continuously been related to the fields of both youth camping and outdoor education.

She is a life-member of the American Camping Association, which she joined first in 1948. She has been active locally and nationally with the ACA, serving on standards, campcraft, and library committees, and as national secretary. She received the Hedley S. Dimock award from ACA in 1973. She is currently on the board of directors of the Fund for Advancement of Camping.

Dr. Ford teaches principles of outdoor education, environmental interpretation, camp administration, and recreation and natural resources. She serves as consultant to many outdoor education programs. Her publications include *Camp Administration* (with L. S. Rodney), *Informal Recreation Activities—A Leaders Guide* (published by ACA), many articles and brochures, and *Principles and Practices of Outdoor Education* to be published by John Wiley & Sons.

SHELL MOUNDS
The ocean was the major source of food supply for the Indian population along the coast in earlier times. Indians camped at various locations along shore where they built fires to cook fish. The shells were discarded piles. When the supply of shell dwindled the Indians moved on. heaps of shells up to 40 feet high

In the words of the cliche, "Which came first, the chicken or the egg?" One might ask, did resident outdoor education contribute to camping or did camping contribute to resident outdoor education? Are the two mutually exclusive or are they, by philosophy, content and methodology, interrelated? In the history of any human endeavor, there is a tendency for some aspects of the enterprise to repeat from time to time and to disappear at other times. A "pendulum" effect may be witnessed as emphasis changes to and from specific elements, programs, philosophies, leaders, objectives, or other aspects. It may be a moot question whether resident outdoor education has made an impact on the camping movement or whether the reverse is true. The two are interrelated, in some ways were conceived simultaneously, and in some ways are inseparable. It may be proposed that resident outdoor education had its birth in the field of organized camping, slowly became a separate entity, and is now realigning with the organized camping movement. Perhaps a few examples will serve to validate this position.

It is relevant to offer a description of camping here so that the reader may understand the similarities and differences between at least two forms of camping and resident outdoor education. To most people, "camping" means living out-of-doors, or a form of housekeeping in the natural environment. It may suggest living in a tent or cabin, sleeping on the ground under the stars, or even living in a motorized camper, recreational vehicle, or travel trailer. "To camp" implies to participate in activities related to the natural resources—such as hiking, fishing, cooking over a fire, building shelters, and erecting teepees or tents. "Camping" generally implies a way of life more simple than that to which the camper will return. Laundry, bathing, clothing, food and personal amenities are simple—often termed primitive—in contrast to the home environment. This concept of camping occurs in small or large groups, often unsponsored by any organization and usually carried out for pure leisure or recreational purpose by groups of friends or relatives with the leaders designated from within the group.

"Organized camping" on the other hand, is defined as a sustained experience under the supervision of trained leaders in the out-of-doors. It is an enterprise sponsored by an identifiable group that solicits campers, provides living accommodations, and offers an education and recreation program under trained leaders. The sponsors are youth-serving agencies, private corporations and individuals, churches, schools, and municipalities.

The organized camping field is made up of day camps (from which campers return home each night), resident camps (where campers stay for a period of several days, weeks or perhaps months), and travel camps (where campers move to different sleeping sites each day by hiking, canoeing, riding, or other means of travel).

The American Camping Association estimates there are 10,000 organized camps in the United States serving an average of 8,000,000 children and thousands of adults each summer. Many of these campers are among the millions of Americans who go camping every year.

Influences of Resident Outdoor

How organized camping and camping in general have been influenced by resident outdoor education is difficult to assess. Several early organized camping programs were concurrently resident outdoor education programs. L. B. Sharp, director of Life Camps, was known as the "father of outdoor education." He started his outdoor education program while directing a summer camp, with the purpose of relating the utilization of knowledge of natural resources to implement outdoor living skills (i.e., camping). Sharp's program entailed shelter building, meal planning and preparation, hikes, explorations, and complete involvement of the campers in the natural world.

As a pioneer in the concepts of decentralized camping and the holistic method of teaching in the early 20s, Sharp first influenced the resident outdoor education program in 1925 through the resident camps. He saw camping as a series of purposefully related experiences in real life situations, hence an educational process. The term "camping education" was accredited to Sharp who continued to influence the field of outdoor education until his death.

William G. Vinal was a camp director and president of the National Association of the Directors of Girls Camps (1920) before he became recognized as an outdoor educator in the 30s, 40s, and 50s. As a college professor, he taught his students through courses which were entitled Biological Field Studies but in a major entitled "Nature Recreation." Much of Vinal's nature recreation content is similar to today's outdoor education and certainly many currently recognized outdoor educators gained their initial exposure to the field, their knowledge, and their objectives from this man.

It is difficult to know whether either Sharp or Vinal influenced their followers as camp directors or as outdoor educators, or whether their impact was *upon* the future camp directors or outdoor educators. The fact remains, early resident outdoor education was greatly influenced by these two camp directors.

These early leaders, either inadvertently or knowingly,

© Phiz Mezey

were so deeply committed to the concepts of educating the total public about the outdoors that they became teachers, consultants, writers, and professors, while they worked with future leaders of youth as well as with youth themselves. Since the commitment to ecological totality is a life-style, it is natural that these people turned to educating leaders to teach all persons, not just those who attended summer camps. It is also natural that their enthusiasm for outdoor learning transcended the summer months and became a twelve-month program in which public school children could participate. These influential leaders then moved from primarily recreational programs to primarily educational programs and a content difference emerged.

Early Outdoor Learning

Prior to the 1920s, most outdoor learning was sponsored under the jurisdiction of the organized camping movement. This was logical, for the camps had the location and the warm season of the year at their disposal and the schools did not. Few teachers were prepared to teach in the out-of-doors and those who were became camp counselors.

It appears that the influence of Sharp and Vinal was not pervasive in the organized camping movement which, like other social movements, passed through several stages. The 1930s saw camping as being recreation-oriented with a "return to nature" element carried over from the 1800s. The camping programs, camp directors, and those writing and teaching about camping were concerned with skills for outdoor living plus the knowledge of flora and fauna for identification purposes. College courses, leadership workshops, and publications on outdoor leadership and summer camps were skill-oriented and "campcraft" (the art of camping) became the vogue. The Life Camps, originally directed by L. B. Sharp, continued to emphasize a total understanding of the natural environment. Camps where students of Vinal counseled were introduced to his similar philosophy. For the most part, however, the organized summer camp programs were not in any way similar to the programs offered by Sharp and Vinal.

In the 1940s, with the exception of war-related program activities (i.e., obstacle courses, first aid, etc.), the camps seemed to focus on what were called curriculum-oriented programs. While a camp might advertise "classes," the education was related to those things *not* taught in the schools. Both summer camps and outdoor schools emphasized a combination of outdoor living skills, real life experiences in the out-of-doors, and simulation of pioneer heritage activities. The outdoor schools often integrated outdoor recreation skills such as archery, fishing, and hunting (i.e., rifle safety) with the regular curriculum along with social living skills. The camps offered no school activities, yet the schools offered many camp activities.

In the 1950s, organized camps were more concerned with social living skills, the group process, and human interaction while the schools, conscious of the need to teach fundamental reading, writing, and mathematics skills, incorporated outdoor education methods and the outdoor school site into teaching the traditional subjects and termed the approach "curriculum adjustment." Possibly during that decade the organized camping field and the resident outdoor education programs were farthest apart. Outdoor recreation skills were disappearing from the resident outdoor schools and the camps continued to focus on activities for outdoor living and activities fostering group processes.

During the early 1960s, a national trend toward developing an understanding of the responsibility toward natural resources evolved. The public read Stewart Udall's *The Quiet Crisis* and denounced the "myth of super-abundance." Aldo Leopold's *Sand County Almanac*, first published in 1948, became required reading for urban planners, landscape architects, recreational resource planners, and many from the public sector. The word "ecology" was voiced often—even by those who knew little of its meaning.

Current Outdoor Education Programs

It is difficult to say how much of the interest in the total understanding of the out-of-doors resulted from resident outdoor education and how much resulted from the ecological awareness developing among the adults. It was probably because of this trend that the youth camp leaders and educators of future youth camp leaders sought ideas for interpreting the environment through recreation programs, and in many instances turned to outdoor educators and to educational materials developed for the schools. Programs originally developed for outdoor education include OBIS (Outdoor Biological Instructional Strategies), the Green Box, the Strands or Web approach of the National Park Service, Project Learning Tree and others which have been modified or left in their original form and utilized by youth camps all over the country. The American Camping Association developed a Camp Ecological Training Program, held workshops, developed model programs for camps, and helped camp directors all over the country to offer programs related to understanding the interrelationship and interrelatedness of all life. The resident outdoor education movement has had a great impact on organized camping through these programs. Many of the consultants for the ACA ecological programs were outside educators who were also active ACA members.

One might ask why the outdoor educator members of ACA had not been vocal before the 1960s. They had been, but until "ecology" became a household word, their voices were not heard. With the national interest in ecology in the 60s, camp directors all over the country gave heed to these people.

One interesting contribution the resident outdoor education program has made to organized camps is an economic one. While some states (particularly Michigan and California) passed enabling acts allowing schools to purchase, maintain, and administer outdoor education sites within or beyond the geographic boundaries of the district, the majority of school resident programs have occurred at camps leased from private, eleemosynary or church organizations. In 1970, the NEA reported that 63 percent of the programs of 702 school systems of over 1,000 children studied in a nation-wide survey used resident sites either on a daily or on a residential basis.

Schools leasing summer resident camps for the purpose of resident outdoor school programs extend the season of potential income from three months to six months or more, depending on the location of the camp and the extent of winterized facilities.

The impact of this extension of camp use can be measured in terms of rental income and can be estimated in terms of longevity of buildings, for there is evidence that buildings which are maintained in a warm, dry condition deteriorate far less rapidly than those which are closed up and left to the hardships of winter. It goes without saying that there are numerous positions in resident summer camps which have become six- to twelve-month positions. Cooks, nurses, maintenance staff, clerks, and in some cases program staff are utilized by school programs in the fall, the spring, and even in the winter where the buildings are winterized or the climate is temperate.

Influences Beyond Organized Camping Programs

Besides the organized youth camp, the influence of the resident outdoor education program may have been felt by those people and programs involved in the activity described earlier as "camping" and in education for camping.

Camping education also appears in programs through organizations that teach camping skills to adults and youth apart from an organized day or resident camp site. Education for camping has been conducted by groups such as: the Sierra Club, municipal recreation departments, youth agencies, college outing clubs, and others. Like the organized camp programs, these organizations started with outdoor skills programs and moved toward the insertion of photography, nature study, ecological awareness and ecological concern programs. Like the camping field, these groups sought ideas to incorporate activities related to ecology concepts into their programs, and they too turned to the programs developed for the schools. Some of these organizations in turn aided the schools in developing material. Particularly obvious are the Audubon Society teachers' manuals for helping urban youth understand the natural world and some of the National Wildlife Federation programs.

Perhaps it is too early to be sure, but it appears that there is a definite trend for resident outdoor education, and organized camping to return to the original teachings of Sharp and Vinal. Learning about and living in the outdoors are inseparable and a holistic approach is the only one that is defensible. Many resident outdoor education programs are adding outdoor pursuits to their curricula while camps are incorporating studies about soil, water, plants and animals.

Whether resident outdoor education contributed more to the camping movement or the camping movement contributed more to resident outdoor education is probably immaterial. The answer is best stated through an ecological concept which outdoor educators all recognize. "Everything is inter-related and inter-dependent." So it is with the outdoor school and camping movements; each has contributed to the other and each is inseparable from the other.

Selected References

The previous material was adapted from *Principles and Practices of Outdoor Education*, by Phyllis M. Ford, a text to be published by John Wiley & Sons, New York.

Chapter 6

IMPACT ON DEVELOPING A SENSE OF COMMUNITY

FIFTY YEARS OF RESIDENT OUTDOOR EDUCATION: 1930-1980

by George W. Donaldson

George W. Donaldson, Ed.D.

Professor of Outdoor Teacher Education
Lorado Taft Field Campus
Northern Illinois University

George W. Donaldson is a "pioneer" in the field of outdoor education. From his initial experience as director of the Lanning School Camp at Trenton State Teachers College in 1943, his lifetime has been spent working in outdoor education during most of the evolutional and developmental years of school camping. His distinguished career includes being the director of the school camping program for Battle Creek, Michigan, during the experimental years with the W. K. Kellogg Foundation (1945-1949), fifteen years as director of the Tyler, Texas Outdoor Laboratory (1949-1964), and professor at the Lorado Taft Field Campus since 1964.

Dr. Donaldson served as the first chairman of the Council on Outdoor Education and Camping and was the first editor of the *Journal of Outdoor Education*. He was the first recipient of both the Reynold Carlson Lecture Award (1976) and the Julian W. Smith Honor Award (1976-1977). He has served as a consultant to over fifty public school systems, colleges and universities, state departments of education, private organizations, and other agencies across the nation and in Canada.

His contributions to professional literature include more than 100 articles that have appeared in publications such as: *School Executive, N.E.A. Journal, Elementary Principal, Journal of Educational Sociology, Camping Magazine,* and *Science and Children.* Dr. Donaldson has authored or co-authored over ten books, pamphlets, and booklets. The most

noted are *School Camping* (1952); *Outdoor Education* (1963/1965); *Perspectives on Outdoor Education* (1972). His wife, Lou, his partner during this long career, helped him to write *Outdoor Education—A Bibliography* (1958); *Outdoor Education in Tyler* (1963); and *Teaching in the Field* (1971).

When such diverse personalities as the late Margaret Mead and Jesse Jackson decry the lack of a sense of community in the entire nation—and especially in the young of that nation—it is high time for educators to listen to what they said. And what they said is of special relevance to educators who work in resident outdoor programs for it is here that a true children's community can be created. This is not to assume that all such centers view the creation of a true children's community as a major objective. Indeed, it has been observed that some, possibly most, resident centers meet few of the characteristics to be detailed in the paragraphs that follow.

Historical perspective is imperative at this point. Outdoor education began in this country as school camping; and school camping, in the late 40s and early 50s, took a holistic approach. It assumed that school camps were children's communities—where children were, for a week or two, both the subject and object of an experiential period of time, removed from the adult-centered community in which they spent most of their lives.

Even the best of today's communities are not ideal settings in which to teach the young a sense of community. Possibly they should be, but any professional educator schooled in community sociology knows that they are not. They are adult-centered, adult-paced, making only token concessions, such as student government and teacher-pupil planning. At best, few schools give heed to the notion that one learns to do by doing—that the way to become a participating citizen in a true community is to practice citizenship in a real community. Since this is practically impossible in the industrial, urbanized, automated, computerized, "hurry-hurry" adult world in which most American children are reared, one of the prime rationales of the early school camping movement was that of removing children from that atmosphere for a period of time, regrettably briefer and briefer these days, and place them in an atmosphere which was child-centered, child-sized, child-planned. These school camps drew upon the philosophies of three ongoing movements in American life: (a) the children's camping movement, rapidly yielding to L. B. Sharp's notion that camps were, by their very nature, educative; (b) the nature study movement, tracing back to the idea of Louis Agassiz, "Study nature, not books"; and (c) the progressive education movement, which was short-lived, but marked a watershed in countless ways on the direction of American education. All three of these streams from which outdoor education flowed were readily observable in L. B. Sharp's Life Camps for children and their adult counterpart, National Camp.

Although decided changes have taken place in what has come to be called residential outdoor education, there remains a residue of the children's community emphasis in most programs. When asked to account for the changes, mainly in the direction of a more academic emphasis in contrast to the holistic approach which stemmed from both National and Life camps and the pre-World War II Kellogg Foundation camps, the writer can only answer that institutions *do* change, but it appears that this particular change was triggered by the general education panic that followed the launching of Sputnik. In the approximate words of the late Earl Kelley: "A wave of guilt swept over the American people and in the familiar scapegoating fashion, they (especially educators) took their guilt out on the least defensible people around—the children." (1) Outdoor education, sad to say, did not entirely escape the panic.

As this is being written, the nation is experiencing, once again, a panic; this time a "back-to-the-basics" movement. Some outdoor education programs have suffered, but not all! San Diego dropped football but kept its long established outdoor program. Intelligent taxpayers will recognize these reactionary movements for just what they are and are not. They are political; they are economic. They have little or no relationship to what is good for children. And whether they are sponsored by Howard Jarvis, the John Birch Society, or a football player who turned politician, they deny the well-established fact that one learns to live by living; that one learns to live richly and fully by living that way, just as one learns to swim *in* the water. Living richly and fully in a children's community is one of the good ways to learn this.

In the author's view, it is not by chance that the programs most influenced by Clear Lake Camp are the programs in which one detects the most community emphasis. At the other extreme are programs that can best be described as outdoor lecture halls, involving mainly the senses of sight and hearing (school senses) with little or no involvement of children except as recipients of words and pointed-out images. The holistic resident outdoor education in contrast displays, on the whole, the following characteristics:

1. *The community is relatively small and homelike.* Its short-time citizens are encouraged to perceive the community's problems and to participate in solving them. No one knows what the per student limit is. (This writer set a limit of two typical classrooms simply because that is about as many children as he can get to know on a personal basis in one week's time.)

Housing, dining, playing, working, and "learning" groups are as small as staffing allows. The Sterling,

Northern Illinois University

Northern Illinois University

Illinois, public schools do this by enlisting the help of a broad range of people in the community. In one session, the president of the school board took night duty in a cabin full of boys, another member of the board taught art, and the school's principal worked in the kitchen and called square dances. Crystal Lake, Illinois, elementary schools are at present so sated with volunteers that they can no longer accept graduate students as aides. Citizen involvement greatly adds to the community atmosphere and goes on in many programs.

2. *The community is permissive in its view of children.* It *lets* children have experiences. It literally lets children work out solutions to all the problems of group life outdoors, imposing only the limits dictated by health and safety. By the same token it *lets* children make mistakes and thereby learn.

3. *The community is an active place.* Entirely too much of a modern child's life is spent sitting—at a school desk or before a television set; this despite the fact that two of the generally accepted characteristics of childhood are energy and activity. L. B. Sharp once said that if the boundless energies of the young could be channeled into constructive directions, we could solve most of our public problems. He made reference to such projects as park maintenance and construction, keeping schools clean and the like.

4. *The community is warmly human.* In a place in which everything is scaled down to be child-sized, an opportunity comes to try for an ideal community, a well-nigh ideal physical environment staffed by highly selected, warm adults. Here the ideal is to do everything— work, play, study, live in an atmosphere of tender,

loving care—by adults and children for adults and children.

5. *The community is a place of work*. Contrary to the common, uninformed notion, children like to work. They do not really like imposed work; the work they like is that for which they know, as well as feel, the need and meaning. The centers which do the most *for* children, rather than practice education by doing, are missing at least two teaching/learning opportunities: a sense of community and meaningful work experience. A commended motto for such a center might be: "We shall work to leave this place better than we found it so that others may use it and enjoy it as we have."

6. *The community is humanistic*. A kindly, supportive atmosphere can be the social climate of this community designed and operated for/with children. To do less is to demonstrate that goodness is something less than good and possible.

7. *The community partakes of spiritual atmosphere*. Here, in a place of natural beauty, can be taught reverence, humility, and the sense of wholeness in nature. A sense of the wholeness of self, in community, can be approached.

8. *The community is a planning community*. This outdoor place, planned for children, can become a place where children can learn to plan for themselves. Children can plan their own programs; in some centers they have been doing so for many years. A sense of community emerges when children are allowed to think and plan for themselves. They can begin to view the place and the experience as theirs, not ours.

9. *The community is a fun place*. Without this final characteristic, all of the ones cited above may appear academic, even dreary. Fun is primary motivation in childhood. Here in the outdoors, removed from the constrictions imposed by the adult world outside, can be created a place and an atmosphere where fun is the watchword. Children need fun, deserve fun; it can become both method and subject when wise, warm adults help them.(2)

The author can think of no better way to cap off this discourse than to quote the following song, written by his wife, which epitomizes a place where they spent fifteen of their happiest—and probably most productive—years. They sang it with thousands of happy children.

© Phiz Mezey

-1-

Camp Tyler is a spot we love,
It's here we work and play.
We do the things that must be done
To live from day to day.
We solve our problems as they come,
We learn from nature's lore
Of all the blessings for mankind
That our earth has in store.

Chorus
Camp Tyler, Camp Tyler,
You're part of everyone
Who's ever lived within your bounds
From rise 'til set of sun.

-2-

The glorious sunrise o'er the lake,
The egret's graceful flight,
The eagle soaring homeward
As come the shades of night,
The flicker of a campfire,
The warmth of friendship true
Will linger in our memories
And keep us part of you.

So, one of the places in the modern world where the young can begin that lifelong task of citizenship, of sense of community, is the resident outdoor education center. This writer makes, again, the motion that we do it!

Selected References

1. Kelley, Earl C., *Education for What Is Real*. New York: Harper and Brothers, 1947.
2. The nine characteristics cited were adapted from two articles prepared by Lou and George Donaldson for *The Camp Fire Girl*, April, 1965, p. 21 and February, 1966, p. 14.

Northern Illinois University

Chapter 7

IMPACT ON TEACHING CONCEPTS

FIFTY YEARS OF RESIDENT OUTDOOR EDUCATION: 1930-1980

by Edward J. Ambry

49

Edward J. Ambry, Ph.D.
President, New Jersey Council for
Environmental Education, Inc.

Edward J. Ambry was a camp counselor and camp director before he entered the field of outdoor education. In 1939 he began working with L. B. Sharp, and continued to serve in a variety of leadership roles in outdoor education.

He was a school psychologist, superintendent of schools, college professor, and for eight years served as the dean of the graduate division at Montclair State College in New Jersey. He directed the New Jersey State School of Conservation for six years. Presently he is professor emeritus at Montclair State College and professor at Rutgers, the University of New Jersey. Currently he serves as president of The New Jersey Council for Environmental Education, Inc., an organization he has directed for the past twelve years.

Dr. Ambry has served on the board of directors of the Outdoor Education Association, Inc., The Conservation Education Association, The Jersey Institute, The New Jersey Association for Environmental Education. He has been engaged as a consultant by The New Jersey Education Association, The U.S. Office of Education, The Tennessee Valley Authority, and numerous outdoor and environmental education organizations.

In 1957 Dr. Ambry received a Certificate of Honor from New York University after serving as president of the School of Education Alumni Association. In 1967 he was awarded the Distinguished Service to Education Award by Newark State College (now Kean College), where Dr. Ambry earned his Bachelor's degree.

A major thrust of educators, whether parents, historians, statesmen, or professional teachers, has been to instill within a younger generation the knowledge, skills, and methods required to form ideas. On the surface, this would not appear to be a formidable task.

Yet, when one stops to examine his or her own ability to form ideas it is amazing to discover how few of us can come close to forming an "original" idea. It has been said that there is "nothing new on earth." Aside from attempting exercises that might result in forming original ideas, let us review our own ability to conceptualize—to have the power, function, and process to form ideas—to work with abstract thoughts—to form opinions.

To perceive through the senses—to see, to hear, and to gain understanding through the perception of the environment around oneself—requires skills and techniques that are difficult to achieve. We all know folks who simply do not see or hear what is happening around them. This requires the mastery of certain interpretive skills which, once mastered and applied, open new vistas of learning and knowledge. It results in a relatively high level of accommodation and adjustment.

To move from the perceiving level of learning to the conceiving level is a giant step. The teaching process used to produce, in the learner, the ability to deal with abstract ideas is a complex process.

If in fact, one claims for resident outdoor education a superior climate for concept formation and learning, then one must examine whether or not this was an objective to be achieved when the outdoor education movement was launched in the 1930s.

Before outdoor educators arrived on the scene in American education there were other educators who experimented with education in outdoor settings. In Athens, Greece, Socrates spent the major part of his life assisting others through his teaching. He talked to young and old, and often he might be seen with a crowd of children about him. He had no schoolhouse. His school was wherever he met persons who were willing to listen to him. Through his simple lessons he was able to have his pupils question their own thoughts and ideas. He caused them to think about the "best" way of living or what the Greeks called "philosophy." His teaching techniques and questioning of authority eventually led government officials to ban his teaching and condemn him to death.

After Socrates was put to death in 399 B.C., his work was carried on by his close friend and pupil, Plato, who became one of the most famous philosophers of Greece. Plato lectured under the shade of the trees that grew around the academy. Both of these prominent educators must have believed that the outdoor setting was superior to indoor teaching situations.

Ruth Benedict, in the classic *Patterns of Culture*, written in 1934, emphasizes the importance of custom and behavior in the development of societies. She stresses that throughout history primitive societies passed on to younger generations their beliefs, skills, and heritage via direct experience, much of which was taught in outdoor settings.

The skills required for survival were demonstrated by the elders and practiced by the youngsters. Beyond this level of learning the elders were also successful in passing on folklore, spiritual learnings, superstitions, and the integration of cultural ideals. They were able to generate thought processes which dealt with abstracts, symbols and imagination. The real measure of success was evident—they survived.

A review of educational development in European countries, and elsewhere, reveals scattered experiments with resident outdoor education; particularly in Germany in the 1700s and 1800s. A similar review of the history of education and the history of camping in America provides evidence that leaders incorporated resident outdoor education experiences in a variety of programs in these same centuries. The programs were not identified as outdoor education, but many of the elements of these programs and their purposes were similar to the early 1930 programs and to some outdoor education programs still in operation today.

The late 1800s and early 1900s was a most productive period of educational thought and experimentation. Prominent educators of this era were engaged in heated debates, extensive investigation, and prolific publication dealing with basic purposes of education and the role of education in American society. These same exciting activities are currently on the American scene and still debated.

At the height of this era certain names emerged and new curricula evolved. Judd, Bagley, Horn, Charters, Cubberley, Briggs, Thorndike, Counts, Bode, Dewey, and Kilpatrick are just a few of the notables. Curriculum ideas such as core, experiential, whole child, traditional, vocational, work-experience, citizenship, progressive, fundamental, personal adjustment, scientific, and others—including camping and outdoor education—were the emerging concepts which sparked the debates.

Charles H. Judd, in the opinion of the writer, typified the extreme point of view that tampering with the traditional curriculum would lead to disasterous consequences. He saw in the progressive education movement a group of cult worshippers who had clearly lost the balancing influences of history and philosophy. That strange entity which they so worshipfully set up as a standard, the whole child, was but an empty verbalism, nowhere to be found. His criticisms of the curriculum emerging in the

1930s would seem to imply the abandonment of all intellectual life. He deplored attempts to displace language and number from their central place in curriculum, and to put in their stead something called activities. Judd was of the opinion that these attempts would prove ineffective and futile.

On the other hand, Werret W. Charters felt that in the subject matter fields, education was more closely articulated with life by using the "activity" approach in curriculum organization and in teaching. John Dewey, in much of his writing, represented the extreme toward the "child centered" curriculum. He decried the repetitious methods used in teaching the so-called "tool" subjects and portrayed this type of teaching as completely divorced from social content and real life. He called for the schools to reorganize the curriculum and to provide settings in which learning could be living and not just preparation for living.

The arguments about proper education and methods of imparting education from one generation to the next were not the exclusive property of educators who flourished at the turn of the 19th century. John Locke (1632-1704), Bishop George Berkeley in 1710 ("Principles of Human Knowledge"), William James (1842-1910), Francis Wayland in 1854 ("Elements of Intellectual Philosophy"), are just a few of the earlier writers who pondered about educational endeavors and methods.

Such books as Thut's, *The Story of Education, Heritage of American Education* by Gross, or *A History of the Problems of Education* by Brubacher; all written in the 1950s and 1960s, provide excellent and adequate reviews of the social and educational scene as outdoor education was launched in the 1930s.

Conditions were ideal in 1930 for new ideas in education. Much of the call for change in education was coming from Teachers College, Columbia University, which assembled on its faculty some of the most forward-thinking educational philosophers.

It was at this time and at this university that a young man named Lloyd B. Sharp enrolled for a doctoral program. This coincided with his employment in January, 1925, as Life's Fresh Air Fund executive director, to reorganize and conduct their camps along the lines of the modern standards and practices found in the best camps.(10)

There is no doubt that L. B. Sharp's program of studies under the direction and influence of John Dewey, William Kilpatrick, E. K. Fretwell, and others at Teachers College produced his original ideas for resident outdoor education experiences in summer camps, elementary, secondary, and higher education. Many of the readers of this book and the author of this section of the book who knew "L. B." will remember his acknowledgements of his

© Donald Rettew

indebtedness to the above professors and others at Columbia University.

There were other camp and educational leaders who were, in 1925-1930, experimenting with new "modern" ideas in camping and education; but it is a matter of record that L. B. Sharp's doctoral dissertation was the first such document to be published in 1930. In it, L. B. Sharp cited several quotations from the writings of Dewey and Kilpatrick to support his thesis . . . "That which can best be learned in the out-of-doors, through direct experience, dealing with native materials and real life situations, should be learned there."

The foundation was laid in 1930 for the promotion of resident outdoor education programs. There appeared to be adequate debate and discussion, at least in the eyes of those educators who leaned toward the philosophic concepts associated with the well-established principle of "learning by doing."

There was little discussion in the early years of the resident outdoor education movement about participants gaining insights into social functioning, democratic living, loyalty, democracy, physical reality, critical thinking, environmental relationships, and barriers of class, race, and territory. To understand any of these would certainly require conceptual learning. However, these areas were not stressed in Sharp's dissertation as outcomes he anticipated from the programs he envisioned.

There appeared in the literature an implied understanding that conceptual learning would take place, and it probably has. However, the justification for these programs stressed objectives such as a more natural educational setting; improved methods of teaching and learning; physical health; understanding of primitive processes; emotional integration; individual growth and development; formation of desirable habits and attitudes; happiness and enjoyment; learning by doing; and self-sufficiency. Being child-centered, rather than merely activity-oriented, it would naturally follow that the emphasis was on the individual's development.

Therefore, the writer, after reviewing much of the early literature and having served as a counselor, leader, director of several resident outdoor education centers, and later as a member of the Board of Directors of The Outdoor Education Association, Inc., presents the proposition that the resident outdoor education movement was not, in fact, conceived as an educational venture in which conceptual development would be accomplished. There is every reason to believe that the early founders of the movement *assumed* that a fairly high level of conceptual teaching and learning would take place in resident outdoor settings, but this is only the writer's interpretation and belief. It may be shared by others who have been active in the field of outdoor education for all or some of the past fifty years.

The May 1947 issue of the *Bulletin of the National Association of Secondary Principals* devoted most of its 200 pages to a comprehensive review of the seventeen-year period of educational experimentation with camping and outdoor education. The writers selected for the series of articles in this issue were chosen from among the outstanding proponents who were advocating the acceptance and expansion of outdoor education.

Sharp, Partridge, Conrad, Masters, Vinal, and others expounded on the progress of the movement and cited success stories, but most of the articles dealt with topics as follows: public support for camping and outdoor education; the integration of teaching aids and direct experience; policies and procedures for operating camps; legal aspects. Goodrich, in one article, came close to dealing with conceptual learning when she described a number of case studies that indicated radical changes in the lives of several youngsters, directly attributed to their experiences in resident outdoor education situations. Throughout *The Bulletin* samples of poetry taken from the materials produced by young people who had participated in resident outdoor education programs revealed that, indeed, these young people had conceived new ideas and were able to organize their thoughts and express themselves adequately and beautifully. For the most part, this seventeen-year review indicated again that workers in this field may have assumed conceptual learning could take place in these programs but did not present evidence that research efforts were mounted to substantiate this assumption. They appeared to be more concerned with process than content.

Again in 1957, a major portion of the May issue of the *Bulletin of the National Association of Secondary Principals* was devoted to an updating of the status of the outdoor education movement. A few of the same persons who wrote articles ten years previously presented new articles; but most of the writers were not those involved in the preparation of the May 1947 *Bulletin*. Again, there was little reference to conceptual learning in this issue, but more justification was placed on programs where the participants were able to learn and to develop skills "in and for the out-of-doors."

Let us pause for a moment to consider a working definition of concept which the writer has taken from a publication entitled, *Putting Subject Matter into Conceptual Form*, by Asahel D. Woodruff, professor at the University of Utah:

A concept is a relatively complete and meaningful idea in the mind of a person. It is an understanding of something. It is his own subjective product of his way of making meaning of things he has seen or otherwise perceived in his experiences. At its most concrete level it is likely to be a mental image of some actual object or event the person has seen. At its most abstract and complex level it is a synthesis of a number of conclusions he has drawn about his experience with particular things.(12)

This definition is not too different from Webster's dictionary which defines concept as: A thought; an opinion; an idea as distinguished from a precept. The writer urges others to search the literature in the field of outdoor education for documentation that education in the out-of-doors produces concept learning. The writer wants to be clearly understood. He is not stating that those exposed to programs offered in residential outdoor education centers do not have repeated opportunities to develop concepts. His challenge to the readers is to produce documentation. It is one thing to "feel" that a program's successes may be amply described in the literature, but it is another thing to search the literature and record the documentation.

Most of the subject matter fields have developed lists of basic concepts to be learned. These appear in publications of learned societies and are usually used in conjunction with efforts to develop curriculum materials. Since outdoor education is most frequently described as process rather than subject oriented, this may explain the lack of literature and research. Perhaps the difficulty lies in the matter of measuring concept formation and learning.

A list of concepts developed by Robert E. Roth as a part of his doctoral dissertation (1969) entitled, "Fundamental Concepts for Environmental Management Education (K-16)" may have been useful in outdoor education. Many of the environmental education programs funded with state and federal funds since 1965 have incorporated the use of resident outdoor education centers, and at least a few of these relatively new programs developed curriculum offerings with emphasis on concept learning. Lists developed by Roth, Stapp, and others for environmental and conservation education in the late 1960s indicated a concern, at that point in time, for focus on concept teaching in programs directly related to outdoor education.

In 1972, The Ohio State University ERIC Information Analysis Center for Science, Mathematics and Environmental Education, published a booklet entitled, "A Review of Research Related to Environmental Education." It represented a review of ninety-four selected publications, including dissertations, books, and brochures, produced between 1930 and 1971. Fifty-seven of the publications dealt with school camping or outdoor education. Only one of these fifty-seven, judging from the titles, was related to student learning, and the study was conducted with college level students. None of the fifty-seven had the word concept in its title. Most appeared to concentrate on administrative problems and organization with a few focused on principles and functions. Two of the documents listed as studies in conservation appeared to be concerned with concept learning and were cited by the editors as "attempts to identify principles and concepts for conservation which resulted in a different form of reference from that existing previously."(8) Several others dealt with concepts, but were devoted largely to identifying, listing, and evaluating the lists of concepts.

Roth wrote a follow-up compilation of studies which was published in 1976. His review of research cited a greater proportion of documents dealing with concepts and concept learning. Again, judging from the titles, only five of the studies dealt with resident outdoor education and none of these placed emphasis on concept learning.(9)

Despite the obvious lack of attention to such a basic consideration as concept learning, as reflected in literature produced by practitioners in outdoor education, the writer has had firsthand experience with programs that have produced knowledgeable young people whose concepts about the meaning of life and the world about them have been drastically influenced by the teaching they were exposed to in resident outdoor education centers. He could name dozens of productive citizens who were students in programs under his direction who would attest to the statement that their resident outdoor education program was more influential in shaping their lives than any other single educational experience. Other leaders in this field could produce similar testimony. Why then, does not more documentation appear in the literature?

Resident outdoor education has expanded in its fifty years. In 1933, Dr. James F. Rogers, of the Office of Education (which was then part of the United States Department of Interior) reported "public school camps in operation in thirty-three cities throughout the country."(5) By 1962 it was estimated that there were "more than 500 school districts" that had developed camps for school use.(1) After 1962, there was another surge of expansion with assistance from federal funds.

Now, in 1980, with programs well established in every state, it is time for outdoor educators to assess the "richness" of their programs by concentrating their attention upon the product—the student. Where are the products of the past fifty years? Who are they? What decisions did they make in their life adjustments which called upon their outdoor education experiences?

After fifty years we may now know enough about administrative procedures and management techniques. We may be ready to move on to examining the kind of product we have produced and could produce in the future.

Perhaps, in 1980, we are ready to follow Walt Whitman's advice:

Now I see the secret of the making of
the best persons, it is to grow in the
open air and eat and sleep with the
earth. Here a great personal deed has
room,
    (Such a deed seizes upon the hearts
    of the whole race of man, Its effusion
    of strength and will overwhelms law
    and mocks all authority and all
    arguments against it.)
Here is the test of wisdom,
Wisdom is not fully tested in schools.
Wisdom cannot be passed from one having it
to another not having it,
Wisdom is of the soul, is not susceptible
of proof, is its own proof—''

Selected References

1. Ambry, Edward J. "An Investigation of the Administrative Problems Related to Resident Outdoor Education Programs in Certain Public Elementary and Secondary Schools." Unpublished doctoral dissertation. Ann Arbor, Michigan Mircofilms, 1964.

2. Benedict, Ruth, *Patterns of Culture*. New York: Penguin Books, Inc., 1946.

3. Brubacher, John S., *A History of the Problems of Education*. New York: McGraw-Hill Book Company, 1966.

4. Haaren, John H., and A. B. Poland, *Famous Men of Greece*. New York: American Book Company, 1904.

5. Jacobson, B., Reavis, William C. and Logsdon, James D. *The Effective School Principle*. Englewood Cliffs, New Jersey: Prentice Hall, Inc., 1963.

6. Lindloff, Johanna M., Camping Committee. *Adventures in Camping*. New York: Johanna M. Lindloff Camp Committee for Public School Children, 1943.

7. Roth, Robert E., "Fundamental Concepts for Environmental Management Education (K-16)." Unpublished doctoral dissertation. Ann Arbor, Michigan: University Microfilms, 1979.

8. Roth, Robert E., and Helgeson, Stanley L. *A Review of Research Related to Environmental Education*. Columbus, Ohio: ERIC Information Analysis Center for Science, Mathematics and Environmental Education, 1972.

9. Roth, Robert E., *A Review of Research Related to Environmental Education, 1973-76*. Columbus, Ohio: ERIC Information Analysis Center for Science, Mathematics, and Environmental Education, 1976.

10. Sharp, Lloyd Burgess. *Education and the Summer Camp*. New York: Columbia University, Teachers College, Bureau of Publications, 1930.

11. Thayer, V. T., *Formative Ideas in American Education, from the Colonial Period to the Present*. New York: Dodd, Mead and Company, 1967.

12. Woodruff, Asahel D., "Putting Subject Matter into Conceptual Form." Unpublished paper for TEAM project meeting. Washington, D.C.: American Association for Colleges of Teacher Education, February 6, 1964.

Chapter 8

IMPACT ON TEACHING VALUES
FIFTY YEARS OF RESIDENT OUTDOOR EDUCATION: 1930-1980

by Clifford E. Knapp

Clifford E. Knapp, Ph.D.
Director, Lorado Taft Field Campus
Northern Illinois University

Clifford Knapp has been a teacher at all levels of education—elementary through graduate schools. He has been associated with outdoor learning programs during almost twenty years of his professional activities. At Southern Illinois University he cooperatively developed an outdoor teacher education program involving local public school youth. In his recent position as director of outdoor education for the Ridgewood Public Schools, he has developed a unique annual program for over five hundred students. He is presently the director of Lorado Taft Field Campus and chairperson of the Outdoor Teacher Education Faculty at Northern Illinois University; the largest and most experienced outdoor education faculty in the nation.

Dr. Knapp has been on the staff of the National Humanistic Education Center since its inception in 1971 where he has taught numerous outdoor workshops for adults and pioneered the Human Relations Youth Adventure Camp for ages 11-14.

He has written numerous journal articles which have appeared in *Instructor, Science and Children, Journal of Outdoor Education*, and many others. He has co-authored an earth science textbook and an environmental bulletin board handbook. He has authored a book on outdoor learning activities and a multi-media wildlife curriculum unit as well as other instructional aides. He has taught outdoor-related courses at Rutgers University, Johnson State College, Montclair State College, Kean College of New Jersey, and Marywood College.

Dr. Knapp's hobbies and interests include woodcarving, fishing, knife collecting, human relations skills, writing, reading, and wilderness traveling.

These are the things I prize
And hold of dearest worth:
Light of the sapphire skies,
Peace of the hills—

Shelter of the forests,
Comfort of the grass
Music of birds
Murmur of little rills,
Shadows of clouds that swiftly pass,

And, after showers
The smell of flowers

And of the good brown earth,
And best of all, along the way,
friendship and mirth.

HENRY VAN DYKE

What outdoor values do you prize and hold of dearest worth? There is little doubt that over the past fifty years of resident outdoor education, many participants have acquired important values. Listening to the sound of the wind through the pines, pausing to smell the honeysuckle fragrance, or stopping to wonder about the name of a mysterious flower—all of these behaviors indicate that values have been affected by past outdoor experience. How did we get the values we hold? How many were purposely taught to us? How can we expand and improve the process of teaching values?

Outdoor education programs can have considerable impact on the teaching of values. In order to explain the truth of this statement, some definitions, assumptions, and examples are necessary. This is the primary purpose of this chapter.

Values guide a person's life and give purpose to living. A value is the belief in the goodness of something which is usually reflected in planned behaviors. For example, I especially value woodcarving and I schedule some time for this hobby throughout the year. The way we thoughtfully use our time is often a mirror of what we value. The number of times we do a particular thing is an indicator of the strength of that value in our lives. What values are reflected in your daily behavior? I used to value highly playing basketball, but now I do less and less. The strength of the "playing basketball" value has diminished in my life. Our values are constantly being displayed to the people around us. What we eat, wear, say, use for transportation, live in, and everything else we do reflects our values. These things are values if we have freely chosen them from a number of alternatives, considered the potential consequences involved, and

reflect pride in our choices.(1) People who are aware of their self power constantly examine their values and seek clarity and consistency. Some values are discarded as we grow and take on new ones, other values travel with us in our journey from birth to death. No one can question that people share some common values and that they also hold many different values. Being aware of, and thoughtfully planning value-reflecting behaviors are important requirements in the definition of a value. One assumption is that people want to behave in the best possible ways for themselves. Even though we all demonstrate certain behaviors that we don't consider to be our values, we are constantly striving to do the best thing for ourselves. How do we learn the values we hold? Undoubtedly, our early upbringing is very influential in shaping our values. The foundation upon which many of our values rest is laid when we are quite young. I'm sure that I value good hard work because my father taught me that this was the best way to put food on the table for my family. I value fishing today because I had many pleasant fishing trips with my boyhood friends. What values do you still hold from your youth? As we grow older, our circle of human contacts expands and we select some new values. When we see people who have different values from ours, we often "try them on for size" to see if we want them for ourselves. We can say then that value development is a dynamic, life-long process. Even if we retain important values for a lifetime, we usually re-examine them and affirm them periodically. We learn values from our environment, picking and choosing those that seem right for us.

Because values are learned, it follows then that they can be taught. The teaching process includes much more than telling somebody something. Teaching is arranging environments for learning. Sometimes we are unaware of the environments we arrange for others, but nevertheless, people learn from them. Many lessons are learned from people who are unaware that they are teaching. Out goal as teachers of values should be to arrange environments that will predictably result in the learning of important values.

How can outdoor education programs contribute to value formation in people? An outdoor education program is, by definition, a designed outdoor experience to meet specific objectives. A good program attempts to arrange as much of the environment as possible in order to influence positive values, concepts, and skills. Each aspect of the program plan must be examined to assess the impact on people's lives. Arranging environments for learning values involves knowledge of people and the skills to implement this knowledge. Being successful still entails an element of chance, because it is impossible to arrange all aspects of the environment. Also, people may react differently to the same value-focused stimulus. The more thought that goes into various aspects of programming, the more predictable the outcomes will be.

The success of a program should be measured by the extent to which participants reflect certain values in their lives. For example, if a student is exposed to a course in bird study and then returns home and shoots hawks, the course was ineffective in influencing positive values about hawks. Outdoor education program success has other constraints, too. Perhaps the most limiting factor has been the amount of time a student is exposed to the outdoors. For many students in schools, their resident outdoor program is limited to five days or less out of a possible 2,300 or more in public education. This is all too little to expect great changes in a value system. Other students are exposed to inexperienced leadership and some negative value environments while participating in resident outdoor education. It is hoped that this chapter will stimulate thought on better ways to create positive value-focused environments.

What are some positive values that outdoor education leaders would like to teach others? Here is a sample list for consideration:

1. Concern for the needs of other human beings;
2. Concern for a positive self image and a healthy body;
3. Care for non-living physical objects and environments;
4. Reverence and respect for living things;
5. Efficient use of food and other energy sources;
6. Appreciation for the inter-relatedness of nature;
7. Enjoyment of outdoor related activities such as hiking, camping, nature photography, canoeing, etc.

What other general values would you like to see others hold about the outdoors?

Each one of the values stated above can be broken down into specific value behaviors. For example:

4. Reverence and respect for living things:

   a. Caring for nature center animals properly and releasing them after short periods in captivity.
   b. Avoiding touching eggs or young birds discovered in nests.
   c. Planting trees or other plants in eroded areas.
   d. Picking plants for nature crafts only when they are found in abundance.
   e. Taking fish or game in season for eating purposes only.
   f. Replacing over-turned logs or rocks to maintain animal habitats.

Even among outdoor educators, there are different opinions about what values to teach. In the above example, some may believe that (a) animals should not be captured at all, or that (d) plants should not be picked for any purpose if they are living, or that (e) fish and game should not be killed under any circumstances.

Whatever the set of desirable values may be, the important point is that outdoor educators must be aware of them and try to arrange as many aspects of the resident environment as possible in order to achieve them.

How may specific values be taught in the resident setting? There is no one way that works best for everyone. One strategy is to attempt to teach the same value by a variety of methods. It is generally agreed that we can teach values by (a) modeling that value (e.g., hiring non-smoking staff if you value longer life expectancy), (b) making and enforcing reasonable rules that limit certain behaviors (e.g., prohibiting littering if you value natural looking areas), (c) coercive techniques such as punishing behaviors that reflect undesirable values (e.g., sending students home if they "raid" another cabin if you value quiet and safety after hours), (d) propagandizing through various media such as books, oral stories, films, songs, posters, (e.g., singing the Smokey Bear song if you value live forests), (e) limiting exposure to only those values deemed desirable (e.g., not visiting a nature center where animals are mistreated if you value humane animal treatment), (f) providing factual information which supports a specific value (e.g., giving ecological reasons why controlled hunting of deer is useful if you value deer hunting), and (g) structuring various value-focused activities that enable students to freely examine specific issues (e.g., asking students to rank the five most important local environmental problems affecting their lives if you value environmental awareness.) Perhaps there are other ways to teach values. It seems likely that all of these seven methods are used to varying degrees in most outdoor education programs. What are the most effective methods for teaching values? The answer to this question is difficult because of the many variables involved. There is, however, a growing body of research which points to the usefulness of (g), structuring various value-focused activities.(2)

Relatively few outdoor lessons have been planned over the years with a value-focused goal. Primarily goals of factual, conceptual, and physical skill development have predominated in outdoor programs in the past. Only recently has there been an interest in, and resources available for, planning value outcomes as the prime purpose of outdoor lessons.

To develop valuing strategies, some simple guidelines should be applied to the planning process:

1. The valuing behavior to be achieved must be clearly stated. (e.g., the student will reduce the amount of water used in washing.)
2. The best method or methods to achieve this value must be selected. (e.g., a contest will be started to find the best "ecology washing techniques.")
3. A "lesson" demonstrating and involving the students in doing the target value must be structured. (e.g., students are asked to brainstorm as many ways as possible to reduce water when washing.)
4. Ample time must be allotted for practice and must be accompanied by supervision checks and evaluation of effectiveness.
5. Follow-up experiences must be planned after returning home in order to reinforce the value. (e.g., assign the recording of water usage in various homes in the student's neighborhood.)

In order to implement value-focused activities, it is important to create a learning atmosphere of trust and safety. People are usually unwilling to discuss their important values under threat of punishment or rejection. Certain value issues do not clearly have a right answer—a number of alternative values may be held without conflicting with established rules and policies. For example, in situations where styrofoam cups are used for drinking, there is no clear-cut "right" answer concerning their use. Value-focused lessons are planned in these controversial areas. A range of different values may be held around an issue and people's opinions may be respected. To insure an atmosphere of trust and safety, people must be given the clear message that it is acceptable to "pass" or refrain from responding without being questioned. They must also be assured that their responses will be accepted cordially and non-judgmentally. This is difficult for some leaders and students to do because of their habit of constant evaluation. People's values need not be aligned exactly for mutual respect to exist. If the atmosphere for value-focused lessons is supportive and promotes acceptance of differences, leaders will usually be effective in achieving value clarity or awareness.

The following value-focused activities are presented as "food for thought" in planning other outdoor value lessons:

Litter Locations

Value focus—Students will leave the outdoors in better shape than when they found it.
Materials needed—Garbage bags filled with specific types of trash (at least 20 pieces of each type). For example, candy wrappers, empty soda cans, toilet paper, can tab tops, plastic six pack rings, bottle caps, etc.
Implementation—Walk to a relatively undisturbed area outdoors and assign groups of students to various spots. Give each group a quantity of a specific type of trash (e.g., bottle caps) and ask them to distribute the objects as though they were litterbugs. Allow them ample creative license for deciding how to litter the area. Upon completion of the littering in various locations, gather the group together and have the litterbugs lead the group to their location. Ask the entire group of students to record the answers to the following questions at each location:

1. On a scale of 1 (not at all) to 10 (very much), indicate how much this scene bothers you.
2. How could this scene harm wildlife?
3. About how long would it take for these objects to decompose and the area appear natural again?
4. What are some reasons a person would throw away this type of litter in the woods?
5. How could we solve this type of litter problem elsewhere?

After these questions are answered and discussion is ended, the whole group picks up every piece of litter at that location. The trash may be saved for use with other groups. After visiting all locations, further analysis of the data may occur to assess the values of the students in regard to littering.

"Tree mendous" Trees

Value focus—Students will care for trees as living things to be protected by not injuring them.
Materials needed—String, tag board identification tags (8½ x 11''), magic markers or crayons, tree conversation question sheets (see below).
Implementation—Ask each student to select a tree and give it a name based upon something that the tree gives to the world, i.e., shade, lumber, fruit, wildlife shelter. (The name should not be the species name for this activity.) Using the Tree Conversation Sheet, ask them to hold a conversation with a tree and record the imagined answers

Northern Illinois University

on the tag board name tag. Be sure they number each answer to correspond with the questions. After finishing, have them tie the identification tag around the tree trunk showing the tree name and the answers written boldly with the magic marker or crayon.

Tree Conversation Sheet

1. How are you doing today _____?
   (tree name)
2. About how long have you been standing there?
3. What gifts do you give to the world?
4. Are you more useful to the world dead or alive?
5. May I cut you down?
6. Why or why not?
7. What are three words that describe you best?
8. When will I see you again?
9. What else would you like to say to me?
10. May I draw your picture?

After each student has recorded the imaginary conversation with a tree, the group reassembles and walks from one tree to the other to share answers to the questions. (If the group is large, the sharing may be done in small groups.) This technique is an excellent way to assess the values of students toward particular trees.

Animal Place Value

Value focus—Students will know that every animal survives best in a particular place and under certain conditions and will not remove them for very long.
Materials needed—Wire coat hangers bent into the shape of circles.
Implementation—Tell the students that they will have an opportunity to closely examine a place where a certain animal lives. To find that place, they are to throw their coat hanger circle wherever they want. They may aim the toss or throw it randomly. When each student has found a place to examine, give them the following instructions:

1. Choose an animal that might live in that place.
2. Can you find any evidence of that animal or the animal itself? (It is not essential to find the animal or its evidence to do this activity.)
3. What conditions within the circle are necessary for the survival of that animal?
4. Imagine each of the life-supporting conditions being removed or polluted one-by-one. How would this affect your animal?
5. What could you do to each circled place to make it better suited as a home for your animal? Do it if you can.

When the students have completed these directions, ask them to share their answers within small groups of 3-5 students.

Beauty Seekers

Value focus—Students will discover beauty in nature by taking the time to observe details in common natural objects.
Materials needed—Clipboards, paper, pencils.
Implementation—Explain that beauty exists every where in common objects if we take the time to find it. Each student is to select an object such as a plant, rock, area of soil, piece of wood, etc., and carefully examine it for ten minutes. An excellent method for examining detail is to sit comfortably with the selected object in view. Then, draw every detail observed with the pencil *without looking at*

the paper. Do not take your eyes from the object throughout the drawing process even if you pause. It does not matter what the drawing looks like because this is an exercise in observing detail and *not* in producing a replica of that object. (Many people are pleasantly surprised at the beauty of the drawing, too.) After the ten-minute observation period, the students answer the following questions:

1. What is beautiful about your object?
2. Is it hard to believe that no other object in the world is exactly like this one?
3. Can you do something to your object to make it more beautiful? If so, what?
4. Examine your object for one minute more. Can you find more beauty in it?
5. Do you believe that ''beauty is within the eye of the beholder?'' If so, how are you like the object you observed?

To Pick or Not to Pick

Value focus—Students will give careful thought before any plant is picked and be able to give acceptable reasons for their actions.
Materials needed—Sheets with questions about picking plants.
Implementation—Some plants can be picked with no danger of becoming scarce in an area and others cannot. Many believe that good conservation practice involves maintaining a variety of plants in an area. In order to decide whether to pick a plant or not, a number of questions can be considered. Distribute the question sheets to the students. The purpose of the sheets is to provide some ideas to ponder before picking a plant. If the answer to a question is ''yes,'' the plant may probably be picked for a particular reason. The student should decide how many ''yeses'' are needed in order to pick that plant. Instruct each student to go outdoors to select a plant and ask the questions. They are to decide whether to pick the plant at the end of the questionning process. (Caution: If there are rare or protected plants in the area and you do not want to risk them being picked, take the students to them first and go through the questions to illustrate why that plant should not be picked.)

Picking Questions
1. Are there more than 100 other plants or plant parts of the same kind in the area?
2. Can you learn something important from picking it that you couldn't learn by leaving it?

3. Can it be made into a useful product that will benefit people in some way?
4. Will the plant be as beautiful as it is now after it is picked?
5. Will the whole plant survive even if I just pick a part of it?
6. Will the area be improved if I pick this plant?
7. Will the plant be saved from destruction if I pick it?
8. Will the plant die soon and decay?
9. Is the plant safe for me to pick?
10. Is it alright to pick this plant even if the answers to all of the above questions were ''yes?''
11. What will you do now? To pick or not to pick, that is the question.

When the group comes together again, the students' values may be assessed from their responses to the questions and from the discussion that follows.

Planning value-focused lessons is not enough if the total environment has not been arranged to teach positive values. Sometimes there are ''hidden'' or unplanned lessons which do not go unnoticed by students. Imagine what values could be learned by the following scenes and practices:

1. Food served on paper plates and beverages served in styrofoam cups.
2. Poorly insulated dwellings in which heat is wasted in cold weather.
3. Tree branches broken by people and trunks carved by people's knives.
4. Lights left on in the staff rooms all day.
5. Soda and candy available at any time of the day.
6. Gory and scary stories told around the campfire by leaders and students.
7. Highly competitive games in which only the physically skilled win.
8. Some staff who are vegetarians because they believe in reducing food energy loss in the food web.
9. Some staff drive cars that get over 30 miles to the gallon.
10. Trails are well maintained and have erosion controls along the way.
11. Vegetable waste is recycled in a compost pile.
12. Leaders bend down along the trail to pick up litter.

These are some ''hidden'' ways in which values are learned. Whether what is learned is intended to be taught is an important question for all outdoor educators to answer.

The goal then for outdoor educators is to carefully and thoughtfully attempt to arrange as much of the environment as possible with an eye toward its impact upon people's values. Outdoor education programs can have a significant impact on the teaching of values. The challenge is there to be accepted or rejected.

. . . You've been asked to think about your values—the things that are really important to you. But if you really hold a value, you must be willing to act on it; if you don't do anything about it, you probably don't hold it as a value at all. It's one thing to be out here and have this experience and think about how you want your life to be. But you can go back to the city and to the same lifestyle—the same activities and values—you had before.

Steve Van Matre(12)

Selected References

1. For futher information about the values clarification process see: *Turning Points* Volumes I and II, edited by Joel Goodman and available from Creative Resources Press, 179 Spring Street, Saratoga Springs, New York 12866 (1978)

2. Kirschenbaum, Howard. *Advanced Value Clarification: A Handbook for Trainers, Counselors and Experienced Teachers.* La Jolla, California: University Associates Press. 1977.

3. Knapp, Clifford E. "Environment: Children Explore Their Values." *Instructor*, Vol. LXXXI, No. 7, March, 1972 , pp. 116-118.

4. Knapp, Clifford E. "Attitudes and Values in Environmental Education." *The Journal of Environmental Education* Vol. 3, No. 4, Summer, 1972, pp. 26-29.

5. Knapp, Clifford E. "Using the Values Strategies with Subject Matter" in Harmin Merrill, et. al. *Clarifying Values Through Subject Matter.* Minneapolis: Winston Press, Inc., 1973. Pp. 116-134.

6. Knapp, Clifford E., "Values Clarification Strategies for the Energy Crisis" *Eco Centric,* Vol. 1, No. 4, January, 1974, Environmental Studies Center, Bowling Green State University, Bowling Green, Ohio 43403.

7. Knapp, Clifford E., and DuShane, Judith. "Clarifying Values for a Better Environment." *Counseling and Values.* Vol. 18 No. 4, Summer, 1974, pp. 266-271.

8 Knapp, Clifford E. "Outdoor Environmental Values Clarification." *The Communicator: Journal of the New York State Outdoor Education Association*, Fall-Winter 1975, Vol. VII. No. 1, pp. 9-11.

9 Knapp, Clifford E. "Open Space Learning Activities." *Science and Children* Vol. 13, No. 7, April, 1976, pp. 10-12.

10. Knapp, Clifford E. and Goodman, Joel. "Making a Difference: Values Clarification and Social Issues." *Turning Points* Vol. II. Saratoga Springs, New York: Creative Resources Press. 1978

11. Knapp, Clifford E. "Values that Make Better Camping." *Camping Magazine.* Vol. 51, No. 5, April, 1979 , pp. 8-9ff.

12. Van Matre, Steve. *Acclimatizing*, Martinsville, Indiana: American Camping Association, 1974.

© Donald Rettew

Chapter 9

IMPACT ON ENVIRONMENTAL ETHICS
FIFTY YEARS OF RESIDENT OUTDOOR EDUCATION: 1930-1980

by Paul A. Yambert

Paul A. Yambert, Ph. D.
Professor of Forestry
Southern Illinois University
 at Carbondale

Paul Yambert has had a life-long interest in teaching and in the environment. He has taught at various levels from seventh grade through doctoral programs and has served as a consultant on the environment. His efforts with the Youth Conservation Corps included co-authoring the *Environmental Education Source Book* and providing much of the material incorporated in the environmental knowledge assessment instrument which has been used nationwide. More recently he has completed a set of three slide-tape modules for the Illinois Institute for Environmental Quality. This series, entitled *Your Environment and You*, is designed to assess environmental knowledge and awareness at the fourth, eighth, and eleventh grade levels.

Paul's current teaching assignment includes courses in environmental interpretation and environmental education. His research efforts are in assessing environmental knowledge and awareness and the degree of compatability between ecological knowledge and environmental ethics.

Dr. Yambert has been the Dean of Outdoor Laboratories for Southern Illinois University, a member of the steering committee for the Camp Ecological Training Program of the American Camping Association, and the Governor's Advisory Committee for Conservation Education. In 1975 he received the Taft Campus Award for Outstanding Contribution to Outdoor Education. He is active in several national organizations such as the Association of Interpretive Naturalists, the Nature Conservancy, and the Illinois Environmental Education Association.

Paul hosts a widely distributed radio program entitled, "The Energy Connection" and is active in solar home design. He has become increasingly involved in environmental interpretive programs for special populations in recent years. His article, "Language and Word Power," published in *What Makes Education Environmental* (1975) has elicited considerable discussion and comment.

"You are an adolescent who moves ahead, opens new territories, conquers the world, and makes mistakes. It is so natural. Every promising adolescent makes mistakes . . . I see you as a promising adolescent who is lost among many dreams and disappointments. Why don't you select your road, set your goals . . . and then direct your actions toward achieving them? Why don't you organize an annual check-up on everything; not only your GNP?"(2)

This excerpt from a "letter to an American" summarizes, or at least alludes to, many of the ethical problems that continue to face outdoor educators after fifty years of "adolescence." In the balance of this chapter an attempt will be made to examine these problems in more detail, to explore the root causes of these problems, and to suggest specific ways in which we may rechart our course.

In order to scrutinize and analyze the impact of outdoor education upon environmental ethics, let us begin by looking at a hypothetical report card.

Pupil-Outdoor Educator
Term—1930-1980

Subject Matter	Grade	Comments
I. Success in teaching isolated facts	A-	Expert at both learning and teaching facts. Some weakness in acquiring facts directly from the environment as contrasted to books
II. Success in teaching integrated facts	C+	Seems to lack capacity for pursuing remote, but significant ramifications
III. Success in teaching values	C-	Does not regularly accept this duty. Does not appear to have developed effective pedagogical techniques
IV. Success in effecting appropriate changes in behavior (i.e., toward ecologically-sound lifestyles)	D-	Does not seem to understand either the requisite definitions or the procedures

Character Traits	Observer's Assessments				
	SA	A	N	D	SD
High degree of environmental concern	X				
High degree of environmental knowledge				X	
Keeps techniques and knowledge current			X		
Demonstrates the type of lifestyle commended in class					X
Strives to prepare students for a post-petroleum world					X
Exhibits an understanding of the social as well as the biological context of eco-system management			X		

SA—Strongly agree   *A*—Agree   *N*—Neutral   *D*—Disagree   *SD*—Strongly disagree

Northern Illinois University

Now, let us examine some of the implications of the report card.

Teaching facts about the environment has clearly been a strong point. Some centers have elaborate and successful programs dedicated to this end. Equally elaborate testing programs have been developed, and there is little doubt that generations of students have developed extensive and detailed factual knowledge about the inhabitants of the biological system which they share.

Teaching about integrated facts, processes, and functions has been a less common and less frequently realized goal. The exceptions to this generalization have been biologically biased so the concept of food chains is likely to be understood, but the concept of entropy is not. The idea that nutrients and energy can both be recycled through an ecosystem is a common misunderstanding resulting from this bias.

Teaching values or, to be more precise, intentionally teaching values is an area for which most outdoor educators are not well equipped. This seems to be true regardless of the teacher's position on the spectrum of desire to teach values, i.e., ranging from the belief that it is imperative to teach values to the belief that it is wrong to teach values. The frequently voiced claim that we teachers should confine ourselves to "the facts" and encourage students to make up their own minds offers the comforting appeal of being both scientific and safe. It also requires acceptance of the belief that facts are useful even if independent of observers, culture, perspectives and eco-systems.

Where We Went Astray

It is patently unfair to blame all the faults of society upon the outdoor education practices and practitioners of the past fifty years. On the other hand, outdoor education had (and retains) a unique potential for effecting changes in attitudes and lifestyles which are ecologically desirable. It is here that we as outdoor educators have failed; not totally, but most significantly. Our sensory approaches have achieved keener awareness, but show little promise stimulating sufficiently sophisticated ecological study. Our stress-challenge programs have achieved success in "training the children of affluence for austerity,"(2) but have tended to place nature in the role of a dispassionate and powerful adversary. Our field biology offerings have at times been models of science teaching, but they have lacked sufficient emphasis on attitudes and values that transcend science.

Our historical treatment of the degradation of the environment has been comprehensive and effective, but it has lacked the proper conceptual framework for avoiding similar problems in the future. We have equipped our students with high quality rearview mirrors and crystal balls that are cracked and crazed.

Nature education went astray in focusing on identification of critters rather than problems. Conservation education went astray in retaining a largely agrarian emphasis (and bias) and in assessing environmental problems almost solely in the context of adequate resource supply. Environmental education has not yet failed, but has visible signs of weakness.

As admitted at the outset, it is unrealistically demanding to expect students and teachers involved in resident outdoor education programs to anticipate and to solve all of the intractable problems of society. We can reasonably expect, however, that after nearly fifty years of resident outdoor education in the United States there would be a significant and informed portion of our citizenry responsive to, and evidencing strong support for, the societal changes that are prerequisite to an orderly transition to a post-petroleum world.

That American education in general and resident outdoor education in particular have failed to effect sufficiently or even significantly the underlying value system in our society seems beyond debate. It may be of value, however, to examine some of the specific failures and causes of failures which retrospect and prospects currently bring into sharp focus.

The first, and possibly the most fundamental, problem seems to be with that enlargement at the anterior terminus of our spinal cord which charitable friends refer to as our brain. Despite the incredible array of capacities which that instrument exhibits, there is a frustrating lack of evidence that we are capable of thinking clearly about remote ramifications. It is tempting to hypothesize that as our brains evolved, there was a premium on fast responses and associated skills in obtaining sufficient food and shelter for the immediate present and near future. That little premium was placed on the ability to anticipate long-run ramifications is comprehensible; but also frightening, since we live in a world where our individual and collective actions, such as flying jet planes or using aerosal sprays, do, in fact, have ramifications throughout the ecosystem.

A second and closely related problem is that our thinking and our teaching have been far too parochial. Debates and demagogery concerning what is good for this city, this state, or this nation abound in a world that is a single ecosystem. We are still acting as if we believed that political boundaries and economic systems are more real, pervasive, important, and immutable than natural laws.

A third problem is our persistence in the belief that teaching facts about the natural world or facts and ecological relationships were goals rather than prerequisites to appropriate changes in lifestyle and philosophy. Harman in discussing "future histories," has pointed out that "the very small percentage of desirable paths to the future . . . appear to require a drastic and prompt shift in the operative values of the society, and a corresponding shift in its institutions."(4) A specific case in point has been our reluctance to inculcate or to accept personally the ethic of frugality. Elise Boulding has suggested that the spaceship image (of which most of us are fond) "can convey the need for frugality even if it is not enough to alter behavior patterns."(1) We have failed to educate our citizenry to what Paul B. Sears has called "one of the least popular aspects of the resource problem—namely the importance of a reasonable frugality."(11)

Another broad area illustrating our commitment to inadequate, if not suicidal, goals is what Harman has referred to as the "industrial state paradigm."(4) Symptoms abound and are uncritically accepted, e.g., progress is defined as technological and economic growth, steady state is equated with stagnation, and acquisitive materialism is accepted as the chief rationale for education. That this system is not sustainable is a fact most of us have blithely persisted in ignoring. Somehow it has penetrated our knowledge, but not our understanding, that "the beginnings of the breakdown of the (industrial state) paradigm are dramatically shown in the fact that its successes underlie all the serious social problems of the day.(4) The scope and nature of these problems is that they do not lend themselves to technological solution. This brings us, once again, to the question of ethics.

We know far less about environmental ethics than it is imperative for us to know. On the other hand, some of our major deficiencies in the area of environmental ethics are becoming increasingly apparent; consequently, we can begin to focus on the types of changes which are needed and the types of programs which can effect these changes.

Most outdoor educators seem to accept, perhaps only tacitly, Leopold's caveat that "in our attempts to make conservation education simple, we have made it trivial."(5) Yet this is the most nearly universal fault of our outdoor education programs. It is as if we believed that we could teach all about food webs and never introduce numbers, all about limiting factors and never discuss energy, or all about ecosystems and never relate them to politics.

Try asking ten people of any age who have participated in outdoor education programs what $E = mc^2$ means. Then ask them in what units E, m, and c are expressed. The urge to comprehend ergs has not been among our heartfelt goals. Similarly, ask the balance of the ten people with whom you are still on speaking terms to estimate the distance between two trees and the weight of a gallon jug of milk. Then ask them to estimate the number of Btu's in a pine board. The fact that energy is the ultimate coin of the realm in the functioning (or non-functioning) of ecosystems has had little impact on outdoor programs. Constraints on the operation of the programs have been far more significant than changes in the program objectives.

A second, and related, weakness of our programs has been the paradoxical one of emphasizing interrelatedness and interdependencies on the one hand and failing to relate to everyday life in the so-called real world on the other hand. Youth learn about the environment and socially acceptable attitudes toward it not only in nature-oriented programs, but also by observing menus, food serving techniques, transportation choices and types of camping gear which are used. The 30 million pounds of plastic drinking straws which are used (and discarded) in the U.S. each year are reminiscent of the old saying about character, "What you are speaks so loudly I cannot hear what you say."

Yet another shortcoming is that most, if not all, of us have been unable to shed the attitudes toward nature that are a part of our cultural inheritance. Among the typical American attitudes toward nature, Paradise has listed:

> Man is the source of all value
> Nature exists only for man's use
> Man's primary purpose is to produce and consume
> Material resources are unlimited
> . . . The most important nation-state is one that can command and use the largest fraction of the world's resources.(10)

In a similar vein, Harman has charcterized the "industrial state paradigm" with such observations as:

> progress defined as technological and economic growth
>
> man seeking control over nature
>
> acquisitive materialism(4)

My point is that the basic soundness of observations such as those quoted above has had little impact upon outdoor education. Inertia including, but certainly not limited to that for which we are responsible, has justified observations such as "there is very little evidence to support the view that an ecological sense penetrates the fundamental modes of human perception."(7)

Another problem with which we have not properly come to grips is that we have not yet reached consensus that changing values is a legitimate function of outdoor educators. To be more precise, we seem to applaud developing sensitivity and awareness as they relate to the stimulating array of sights, smells, sounds, feels, and tastes that pervade our environment. However, most of us have shied away from relating the ecological truths to reasonable assessments of Marxism, free enterprise, democracy, abortion, and religion. It is no coincidence that economical, ecological, and ecumenical have a common Greek root (oikos), but some of us do not yet feel comfortable including in our 'nature' programs such assertions as "justification of a technological arrogance toward nature on the basis of dividends and profits is not just bad economics—it is basically an immoral act."(7) Why should we be embarrassed in discussing the need for what Miller has called a "caring explosion" and not embarrassed in discussing a knowledge explosion or population explosion? Are these explosions not all interrelated and all parts of a single ecosystem?

One of the ways in which we outdoor educators are *not* unique is that we are, to a large extent, prisoners of our culture. We all share to varying, but considerable, degrees the eccentricities and idiosyncrasies of our times. From the standpoint of environmental ethics this has flawed our vision as well as our performance. At the heart of any viable system of environmental ethics is an holistic perspective, but American society is more accurately characterized by a preoccupation with individual components and processes of the social/biological ecosystem. For purposes of elucidation, it may be helpful to examine some of our more obvious narrow preoccupations and their ramifications.

Econocentrism. Despite widespread dissatisfaction with decisions reached by relying solely upon the analytical tools of economics, we have yet to inculcate an environmental ethic which consistently causes us to transcend the economic in charting the course for our individual and collective actions. Fackre has defined econocentrism more narrowly as "a confident faith in economic growth as the pole star of society." (3) It is both strange and unfortunate that we who should most thoroughly comprehend concepts such as homeostasis and stability in the biological world have not yet begun to teach and to live as though we understood the validity of these concepts in our socio-economic world as well.

In a world of finite resources, finite assimilative capacities and finite rates of energy flow, we can no longer excuse ourselves for giving homeostasis a pejorative connotation more closely linked to stagnation than to balance.

Technocentrism. A common lament among outdoor educators is that "though we have enough science and technology to put a man on the moon, we cannot maintain a decent environment in the United States." As Murdock and Connell have pointed out, "The implicit premise here seems clear: the solution to our ecological crisis is technological."(8) It is not necessary to be a Luddite to recognize the irony in our tacit assumption that the solution be solved, largely, by technology. Yet this assumption has pervaded our thinking and our teaching to such an extent that alternate solutions are seldom considered. Furthermore, the fact that some problems are simply not at all amenable to technological solution remains either unknown or almost totally ignored.

The twenty-four hour living, which has been a unique feature of resident outdoor education, has the prerequisites for instilling thought patterns and life styles that exhibit less tradition and more potential than those currently in vogue. We have yet to capitalize upon this singular opportunity.

Synchronocentrism. To some extent every generation is a "now generation" if by that we mean "preoccupied with the present." Lack of knowledge of the importance

Northern Illinois University

of the past and insufficient experience to appreciate fully the significance of the future are characteristics that stereotype the adolescents of any culture and any era. Perhaps the fact that many of the outdoor education experiences that we provide are of short duration, only peripherally related to the scope and sequence of the classroom has caused us to fail to expand significantly the time frame with which our students are concerned. Unless we plan outdoor activities to provide a far broader perspective of time, we shall continue to rate poor marks—particularly from our progeny. Synchronocentrism, coupled with technocentrism, has led to a complacency that borders on arrogance. This common wisdom seems to be that not only will our problems (energy, population, pollution, etc.) be solved, but they will be solved with very little discomfort, inconvenience, or effort on our part. The moral of "the twenty-ninth day" has escaped lesson plans and escaped our students.

Patriocentrism. The so-called energy crisis (really a power crisis) has served as a focal point for numerous environmental lessons, but has not yet persuaded us that we all live in a single world ecosystem and that our problems and their solutions exist in that broader context. For purposes of clarification and convenience, we outdoor educators have used field trips and local case studies with considerable success; but we have failed to instill the understanding that little watersheds are invariably parts of larger watersheds and that neither the major problems nor their solutions can be found within the confines of political boundaries.

From the foregoing discussion it, no doubt, has become clear to the reader that it is the author's opinion our environment is not in good condition and that, despite numerous official and unofficial efforts to reverse the trend, the deterioration, except in isolated instances, continues at a significant and appalling rate.

Since much of the outdoor education effort has been focused upon developing awareness, concern, and action on the part of our students and ourselves, it would be difficult to claim that we have succeeded. We may reasonably discuss whether the job could have been (or can be) done, the extent to which we share the blame with other environmentally-oriented problems, or what our degree of success or failure has been. Few, however, would dispute that we have not really succeeded.

One approach to measuring our collective success or failure in instilling environmental ethics is the simple, but revealing, technique of assessing the current quality of our environment and noting the trends which currently prevail in enhancing or degrading the environment. Since 1969 the National Wildlife Federation has been providing us with an assessment of this type that is known as the E(nvironmental) Q(uality) Index. Their recent summary for the 1969-1979 decade may be paraphrased as follows:

> Wildlife—down
> Air—up
> Soil—down
> Minerals—down
> Forest—same
> Living Space—down
> Water—down(9)

If we accept the contention that ethics have meaning only in the context of action, it is difficult to claim that our outdoor education programs have effected significant changes in lifestyle which, in turn, have effected significant improvements in the major components of our environment.

Where Do We Go from Here?

It seems inevitable and, in my opinion, desirable that outdoor education program will continue to explore and utilize a multitude of techniques. As objectives toward which these techniques may be directed, it is convenient to explore three broad areas, namely, *attitudes, knowledge,* and *behavior.* In briefly examining each of these, specific examples of recommended goals will be offered, but no attempt will be made to provide an exhaustive list of desirable goals.

Knowledge. Our attempts to impart knowledge of considerable scope and depth should place increasing emphasis upon gaining understanding of ecological ramifications both temporal and spatial, throughout our ecosystem. We have learned and taught that "it is impossible to do only one thing," but we have not yet succeeded in getting this beyond the mere intellectual recognition stage. That is, it is generally something students may answer correctly on a quiz, but not something which will influence their choice of fabrics, foods or furniture. In short, the understanding has not yet become sufficiently visceral or sufficiently sophisticated to have any significant or demonstrable effect on the welfare of the ecosystem.

Attitudes. Teaching attitudes and values in an area in which we have lacked common goals, relevant knowledge, specialized skills, and sufficient commitment.

Some of us are still idealistically, but naively, arguing that our job is limited to teaching "facts;" and that the students, on their own, will arrive at proper conclusions, develop acceptable attitudes and exhibit ecologically responsible behavior patterns. It is quite an understatement to suggest that everyday observations do not support this belief. Furthermore we can readily find some of the reasons why such a belief is ill-founded.

We need to learn and to put into practice more of the growing knowledge which is available on how attitudes are formed (e.g., Fishbein) and the stages of moral maturation of which a personal system of environmental ethics is a part (e.g., Kohlberg).

Just as all education is, to some extent, environmental; all attempts at education apparently influence formation of attitudes—whether or not they are planned to do so. It will behoove us then, to become more professional in our understanding of attitude formation and the linkages among knowledge, attitudes, and behavior.

Behavior. Knowledge and attitude do not impact directly upon the environment; behavior does. Consequently we need to find means of promptly and permanently effecting "eco-compatible" behavior. The common wisdom that knowledge influences attitudes and attitudes influence behavior is now seriously challenged. It is too slow and too ineffective to be relied upon. More importantly it is probably not true and quite possibly backwards. There is increasing evidence that changing behaviors, assuming an educational environment, can not only directly reduce environmental impact but also indirectly result in modified attitudes and revised knowledge. A homely example may clarify this abstraction. Suppose some campers aid in the construction of a spiked board which, when properly weighted, can provide a reasonably accurate measure of the softness of the earth. Suppose also that the spiked board is then used to determine whether or not the soil is sufficiently firm to allow horseback riding on the trails without causing unconscionable environmental impact. Thus we not only have a system for modifying behavior in an acceptable, effective, and prompt way; but we also have a behavioral stepping stone for developing attitudes and knowledge.

Proposed Criteria for Evaluating Future Progress

Leopold did not hesitate to define "good" in terms of our impact upon the environment. He stated simply (and elegantly) that something is good if it increases the stability, integrity or beauty of the environment and bad if it does otherwise.(5)

Miller in his plea for earthmanship ethics provides some insights both into where we have been and where we need to go in our cultural and ecological evolution. He characterizes both the Frontier/Industrial stage from which we are emerging and the Spaceship stage

Northern Illinois University

toward which we are moving as being essentially man-versus-nature in their orientation. Earthmanship, his ultimate stage, is characterized by an emphasis on man *and* nature in a form of symbiosis. He challenges those of us who have believed in the simple prescription of more and better science by arguing that our greatest deficiency is that we are still without "a sense of ought."(7)

In my own work I have found a matrix which seems to be valid, comprehensible and (at least moderately) useful. It is based upon studies which demonstrate what most of us believed prior to such efforts at "proof;" namely, that most us attach far greater value to the here and now than to the there and then. In economic terms, we tend to have a high time discount rate. In sociological terms we place far higher value on our own nearby territory than that of others who are remote geographically. To these temporal and spatial concerns it seems appropriate to add a concern of kinship. How big is our concept of "we?" We in our state? We of the same color? We people? We animals? We living things? We components of the ecosystem? We can summarize these concepts as temporal, spatial, and congenerous. My thesis is that we can gain useful insights into the sophistication of our system of environmental ethics (and, therefore, into the probability of success) by ascertaining the extent to which we have been able to extend the horizons of our continuing concern from the here, now, and me, toward the there, then, and we. Our position on these abstract continuums will, in all probability, determine our position in the ecosystem of the future.

Selected References

1. Boulding, Elise. "Myopic View from Olympus." In *Ecology and the Quality of Life*, pp. 191-201. Edited by Sylvan J. Kaplan and Evelyn Kivy-Rosenberg. Springfield, Illinois: Charles C. Thomas, 1973.
2. Doxiadis, C. A. "Three Letters to An American." *Daedalus*, Vol. 101. No. 4 of the Proceedings of the American Academy of Science, Fall 1972, p. 182.
3. Fackre, Gabriel. "Ecology and Theology." In *Western Man and Environmental Ethics*, pp. 116-131. Edited by Ian G. Barbour. Menlo Park, California: Addison-Wesley Publishing Company, 1973.
4. Harman, Willis. "Planning Amid Forces for Institutional Change." In *Ecology and the Quality of Life,* pp. 235-247. Edited by Sylvan J. Kaplan and Evelyn Kivy-Rosenberg. Springfield, Illinois: Charles C. Thomas, 1973.
5. Leopold, Aldo. *A Sand County Almanac and Sketches Here and There.* New York: Oxford University Press, 1949.
6. Means, Richard. *The Ethical Imperative.* Garden City, New York: Doubleday and Company, Inc., 1969.
7. Miller, G. Tyler. *Living in the Environment—Concepts, Problems and Alternatives.* Belmont, California: Wadsworth Publishing Company, 1975.
8. Murdock, William and Connell, Joseph. "All About Ecology." In *Western Man and Environmental Ethics*, pp. 156-170. Edited by Ian G. Barbour. Menlo Park, California: Addison-Wesley Publishing Company, 1973.
9. *National Wildlife's 1978 Environmental Quality Index.* Washington, D.C.: National Wildlife Federation, 1978.
10. Paradise, Scott. "The Vandal Ideology." *The Nation*, December 22, 1969, pp. 730-732.
11. Sears, Paul B. "Ethics, Aesthetics and the Balance of Nature." In *Perspectives on Conservation*, pp. 106-111. Edited by Henry Jarrett. Baltimore: John Hopkins Press, 1958.

San Francisco State University

Chapter 10

IMPACT ON LEISURE ACTIVITIES

FIFTY YEARS OF RESIDENT OUTDOOR EDUCATION: 1930-1980

by Oswald H. Goering

Oswald H. Goering, Re.D.
Professor of Education
Director, Kauffman Museum
Bethel College

After receiving his doctorate in recreation from Indiana University, Oswald H. Goering served for the next four years as dean of men at Bethel College, North Newton, Kansas. He joined the faculty at Northern Illinois University in 1958 and was appointed as chairman of the faculty of Outdoor Teacher Education at the Lorado Taft Field Campus in 1977. In 1979 he returned to Bethel College as the director of the Kauffman Museum and as a professor of education.

Dr. Goering has traveled extensively in Europe and South America and participated in teaching assignments in foreign countries, including Germany and Puerto Rico. He has co-authored two books: *A Leader's Guide to Nature-Oriented Activities* (1965) with Betty van der Smissen and *Perspectives in Outdoor Education* (1972) with George Donaldson.

Dr. Goering served as chairman of the Council on Outdoor Education in 1970-1971 and was the recipient of the Julian W. Smith Award at its 1978 National Outdoor Education Conference in Arizona. He has been active in professional organizations such as the American Alliance for Health, Physical Education and Recreation, and the American Camping Association.

In order to understand the impact that fifty years of outdoor education have had on leisure activities, it is necessary to explore some of the changes that have taken place during this period of time as well as some of the reasons for these changes. From the very beginning, the people of the United States have had a natural inclination to participate in outdoor activities. During the pioneer era, hunting and fishing were an inexpensive means of providing food for the family and were an important part of the family financial structure. Of equal importance was the challenge that these activities offered in the matching of a person's wit and skill with that of animals and nature. Survival skills were a necessary part of this situation, and so one learned to live off the land, find shelter when needed, build fires in adverse conditions, and to find one's way when lost.

As America became settled and the industrial revolution set in, the life-styles of its people drastically changed. During the pioneer days approximately 90 percent of the population lived in a rural area. They were involved with agriculture and had close contact with the natural environment. With increased technology and better farming practices, the size of farms grew, and more of the population found itself living in suburbs where the employment possibilities were better. Thus the major portion of the population has shifted from direct involvement with the land to where today 90 percent of the people live in an urban environment with minimal contact with the soil and the outdoors. In a relatively short time, this nation has seen its people move from living on the land to living on concrete and asphalt.

One of the great changes brought about by the industrial revolution is the amount of leisure time that the average American has available today as compared to fifty years ago. For many workers the thirty-five hour week is a reality and an increasing number of companies are experimenting with the four-day workweek. Not only has the week been shortened, but an increasingly larger percentage of the people hold sedentary positions finding it necessary, for health reasons, to participate in active physical activity during their leisure time. This simply means that Americans have more time and energy available to do the things that they want to do than they ever had before. While this seems to be a blessing, it also has brought about its problems in that many people are not prepared to take advantage of the opportunities afforded by this newfound time. Historically the emphasis in our education system has been on how to earn a living rather than on how to live. Colleges and universities, in their attempt to attract students, stressed how much larger an income a college graduate can expect than the non-college person. The result is that many people are frustrated in having time available, but not knowing how to plan for and to enjoy their leisure. They often participate in activities that require the least amount of effort, which too frequently is turning on the television set rather than to become involved in a creative activity that is truly refreshing and recreative.

Social Life, Travel, Leisure Time Activities Changed

The technological advances in transportation have drastically changed the way people live and what they do in their leisure time. Not only do Americans have longer vacation periods, but with the modern transportation systems there is no place in this country that is more than a few hours away. Travel costs are relatively low, and most people have the opportunity to travel from one end of the country to the other to visit friends or to explore a different topography and climate. The modern automobile is designed so they can travel on the coldest of winter days or cross deserts on the hottest of summer days in comfort. It is not unusual for people to travel thousands of miles across the country during a one- or two-week vacation period.

The advancement of the automobile has had another effect which has drastically changed the nature of social life. Americans were generally confined to their homes and local communities for their social and recreational activities. Today nothing is thought of traveling forty or fifty miles to see a movie, to visit friends, or to shop for a few hours in a larger city. The availability of all-terrain vehicles such as the four-wheel drive trucks, snowmobiles, dune buggies, and motorcycles make it possible to get to remote areas that just a few years ago were accessible only to the most hardy hikers and campers.

The improvements and availability of outdoor recreation equipment has opened new opportunities for participation which were not available to the average American a few years ago. The fisherman has an assortment of rods and reels, boats, motors, and sonar fish locating devices. The hunter has clothing to keep him warm so that he can be in the outdoors for extended periods of time in the coldest weather. Outdoor recreation specialty stores have greatly increased in numbers, and the finest equipment is now available in small towns and in the most remote areas.

One of the biggest changes has been in the attitudes of the people toward moral and social values. Fifty years ago the Puritan work ethic was the primary operating philosophy. Idleness was usually accompanied by guilt feelings, and if one was not utilizing his time to produce something or preparing himself to become more productive, he was "sinning" and wasting his opportunities.

With the increased amount of leisure time, has come the acceptance of the fact that a person, for his mental and physical health, needs to relax and to participate in diversionary activities which may or may not be productive but are enjoyable. The emphasis upon accumulating material goods as a lifetime objective is not nearly as widely accepted today as it was at one time, and increasing numbers of people are searching for other meanings to life.

The liberalization of attitudes toward marriage and sex has also had an impact upon the participation in outdoor activities by Americans. A few years ago it was impossible for a group composed of unmarried boys and girls to participate in a camping or backpacking experience without being suspect. Today such groups camping and traveling all over the United States is accepted as nothing unusual.

The celebration of Earth Day and the gasoline shortage of 1975 combined to confront the American people with the problem of the rapid depletion of natural resources. Suddenly everyone was concerned about the quality of our streams and air. Popular support for projects such as collecting and recycling glass, paper, and aluminum grew rapidly. Groups emerged that were interested in saving prairies and other natural environments. It is interesting to note that during this time there was enthusiasm for the possibility of developing a lead-free gasoline that would help the air pollution problem—until it was discovered that this gasoline cost slightly more than regular gasoline. It is a sad commentary that people seem to vocally back a cause until it affects their pocketbook or limits their mobility. Too many of the people who were strong supporters of environmental concerns today have their cars illegally modified, removing anti-pollution devices so that they can burn the cheaper gasoline.

Interest, Participation in Outdoor Activities Increasing

America is experiencing increased interest and participation in outdoor leisure activities by people in all walks of life. The overfilled campgrounds in our state and national parks are evidence of this interest. During the summer months, the rock climbing areas are so filled with climbers and ropes that one needs to go early to find good places. Cross-country skiing is one of the most rapidly growing sports today. Include in this list the hunter, fisher, snowmobiler, hiker, and one begins to get a small feeling of the immense numbers involved in outdoor activities. The backpacking trails are so filled with hikers that there is genuine concern about the

erosion of the trails and the effects of overuse on the campsites. Fortunately much emphasis is now being placed on "no-trace camping" while just a few years ago we were teaching skills like lashing, selective cutting of saplings for shelter and camp construction, and fire-building. Today the cutting of live plants is forbidden in most areas, and the building of open fires has been greatly restricted. The camper and backpacker of tomorrow will be carrying his stove and fuel on which to do his cooking.

A number of historic events have influenced the possibilities of outdoor recreation activities and increased the natural areas available to the public for these pursuits. Better known among these are the establishment of the National Park System and the U.S. Forest Service. The Wilderness Act passed by Congress in 1964 set aside large numbers of acres to be maintained in a wilderness state to be available to and enjoyed by present and future generations. The formation of the Bureau of Outdoor Recreation and the production of a Nationwide Outdoor Recreation Plan requested by Senator Henry Jackson were influential. Also making major contributions are the Outward Bound schools, the National Outdoor Leadership School, and the New Games Foundation.

The Wilderness Act marks an important milestone in the preservation of natural wilderness areas for the use and enjoyment of the American people. Some nine million acres have been set aside as part of the National Wilderness Preservation System. These areas were undeveloped federal lands, which now offer Americans the opportunity to participate in activities in primitive areas and enjoy the solitude that they offer. Motorized vehicles usually are not permitted in these areas.

The Bureau of Outdoor Recreation was established in 1962 and is responsible for providing outdoor opportunities for the American people now and in the future. The bureau is the coordinating agency responsible for taking the lead to recommend and to guide the government's recreation policies, planning, technical assistance, and research. However, its responsibilities do not include the management of land, water, or recreation areas. The bureau's primary responsibilities are to:

1. Identify critical outdoor recreation problems.
2. Recommend viable solutions to these problems.
3. Propose federal, state, local, and private actions.

The bureau does have funds available to assist states in the development of comprehensive outdoor recreation plans. The state of Illinois completed such a cooperatively funded plan in 1974. These funds are also used to match state funds for the acquisition and

© Phiz Mezey

development of outdoor recreation areas. The bureau works cooperatively with the National Park Service, Bureau of Sport and Fishes, U.S. Forest Service, and the Bureau of Land Management.

The Outward Bound schools began in England during World War II as a result of wartime needs. The German U-boat activity was at its height, and many lives were being lost as seamen faced emergency situations. A merchant skipper, named Lawrence Holt, noticed that life loss among the untested young recruits was much higher than among the seasoned seamen. In an effort to strengthen the spirit of these young men against unnecessary defeatism, both mental and physical, he enlisted a former German schoolmaster, Kurt Hahn, and together, in 1941, they established the Aberdovey Sea School in a rocky, windswept port in Wales and called it "Outward Bound." By placing the students into unusual stress situations, they were able to instill in them the desired attributes of the seasoned seamen, and the life loss dropped drastically.

After the war, it was decided that the school had peacetime applications as well, and soon new schools were opened throughout the world. Countless other out-door programs are using adaptations of their activities and approach. The first Outward Bound school to be opened in the United States was in Colorado in 1962; today there are six Outward Bound schools in the country. While each school has its unique activities, their purpose and philosophy are the same. They want individuals to learn more about themselves and their abilities and thus build self-respect and self-confidence. This is usually done by having the participants take part in a four-week program designed to confront the individual with stress and challenge situations. In Colorado, this includes mountaineering (climbing), an obstacle ropes course, initiative tasks, group problem solving situations, and a solo experience. Throughout the course, time is given for introspection, self-examination, and contemplation along with the physical challenges. Readings and discussions set the tone for the experience which gradually builds to a climax with the "solo" when the individual spends three days in solitude reflecting upon his experiences and his relationship with the other members of his patrol.

Many educators agree with the basic philosophy and objectives of the Outward Bound schools. There is a great need among our students to develop a better self-image and, too frequently, children go through school without being confronted with any real physical challenges. Many outdoor education programs in the United States and Canada are now including stress activities in their programs. Children seem to have a natural interest and desire to participate in such activities and are highly motivated.

While it is difficult to assess the contribution made by the Outward Bound schools, there is no question they have had a tremendous impact on the nature of the activities now used in outdoor education centers and on the increased popularity of participation in stress activities by both youth and adults. Interest in rock climbing, white water canoeing, backpacking, wilderness camping, spelunking, and cross-country skiing certainly has been helped by the programs of the Outward Bound schools.

The National Outdoor Leadership School, located in Lander, Wyoming, was founded in 1965 by Paul Petzoldt, who was formerly an instructor in the Colorado Outward Bound school. The program focuses on studying and teaching techniques of practical conservation, mountaineering, and outdoor leadership. The school offers courses lasting from two to five weeks for people with a wide range of age and experience. Survival and outdoor living skills are stressed. Currently emphasis is being placed upon the "Wilderness Certification" program.

The heart of the certification program is to educate all wilderness users in practical conservation techniques, which will permit them to enjoy a primitive area and leave it in its natural state. The number of people participating in activities in wilderness areas has rapidly increased, and many of the natural resources and beauty are being marred and depleted by well-meaning but unknowledgeable backpackers and campers. In order to protect these areas the government is considering several courses of action including: *(a)* required training and certification of wilderness users; *(b)* establishing a quota system for wilderness areas; and *(c)* the placement of residential conservation teachers in the back-country. The certification program has the possibility of making a great contribution to outdoor education programs in the preparation of leaders for activities in wilderness areas.

Another program that has greatly benefited the hikers and backpackers is the National Trails System Act passed by Congress in 1968. Primarily two trails were identified: the Appalachian Trail and the Pacific Crest Trail. These trails are scenic in nature, but have been subjected to such heavy use during the last few years that erosion has become a serious problem. The

Appalachian Trail extends 2,044 miles along the Appalachian mountain range from Georgia to Maine. It is administered by the National Park Service. The Pacific Crest Trail follows the mountain ranges of the west coast beginning in California on the Mexican border and reaching through the states of Oregon and Washington to the Canadian border. It covers a distance of 2,3! miles. The U.S. Forest Service administers this trail. Many lesser and local hiking trails have been establishe and are being utilized by an ever increasing number of people.

The New Games Foundation began in 1966 on the San Francisco State University campus when Stewart Brand was asked to provide activities for a meeting of the War Resisters League. The emphasis from the beginning was to get as many people as possible to participate, just for the enjoyment they receive, in noncompetitive play. Its motto has been "Play Hard, Play Fair, Nobody Hurt." The atmosphere is conductive to creating spontaneity and active participation. Rules of games can be changed to fit the situation and frequently score is not kept. The foundation sponsors leadership training workshops throughout the country and has published *The New Games Book* which is filled with suggestions for noncompetitive activities. Their influence has changed much of the emphasis in physical education programs i many schools and universities as well as programs in sum mer camps and outdoor education centers.

In 1974 a Nationwide Outdoor Recreation Plan was developed by the Environmental Policy Division of the Congressional Research Service of the Library of Congress at the request of Senator Henry M. Jackson, chairman of the Committee on Interior and Insular Affairs. This plan relies heavily upon the research conducted by the Bureau of Outdoor Recreation in 1960. It indicates that there will be four times as many people participating in outdoor recreation activities in the year 2000 as there were in 1960. If our natural and wilderness areas are already being destroyed by inept campers and overuse, then the acquisition of additiona areas and the providing the users of necessary skills become paramount concerns.

Outdoor Education Project Established

During the 1950s, the "Outdoor Education Project" was established through the cooperation of the American Association of Health, Physical Education, and Recreation and the manufacturers of outdoor recreation equipment. Dr. Julian W. Smith of Michigan State Un versity served as its director until his death in 1975. During this time he organized and sponsored many Ou door Education workshops that featured archery, shooting, and casting skills as well as emphasizing the concept of utilizing the outdoors to achieve other educational objectives. The formation of the Council on Outdoor Education and Camping continued to bring educators together to discuss and promote outdoor education. As a direct result of these workshops and council activities, including national conferences, many teachers acquired the necessary skills and interest to institute outdoor recreation-education programs in their schools and classes.

While it is difficult to assess and to pinpoint the contributions that fifty years of resident outdoor education have had on American education we can get some insight by examining the changes that have come into the physical education programs emphasizing lifetime outdoor sports and skills. There also have been an

increasing number of outdoor clubs formed which focus on the outdoor recreation activities previously discussed in this chapter. This, however, is only the beginning, and much needs to be done if we are to reach the desirable outcomes and attitudes.

It is interesting to note that one of the primary objectives of outdoor education programs has been to help as many of the students as possible to develop an awareness and appreciation of the materials and processes that are found in the outdoors. If the proper attitudes and appreciations are formed, then their interest in exploring the out-of-doors will continue throughout life. It is not possible for a person to live his life to the fullest if he has not had the opportunity to develop these appreciations of the natural environment; he has a void in his life in the same way as a person who

Ball State Teachers College

has not had the opportunity to learn to appreciate good music or art. Success in reaching this objective, to develop an interest and appreciation for the outdoors, seems to contribute directly to the problem of not having sufficient areas to meet the ever increasing demands of the public. Overuse and the fact that many of the users do not have the skills and knowledge neccessary to protect the natural environment threaten the very existence of wilderness areas. The great challenge now confronting educators is not how to get people interested in the outdoors, but rather how to adequately prepare them so that they can enjoy their experiences in the natural environment to the fullest without destroying it.

Selected References

1. Fluegelman, Andrew, editor. *The New Games Book*. Garden City N.Y.: Doubleday and Company, 1976.
2. Hogan, J. M. *Impelled Into Experiences, The Story of the Outward Bound Schools*. London: E.P. Publishing Company, Limited, 1963.
3. Illinois Department of Conservation. *Illinois Outdoor Recreation*. Springfield, Illinois: Department of Conservation, 1974.
4. Jackson, Henry M., *A Nationwide Outdoor Recreation Plan*. Washington, D.C.: U.S. Government Printing Office, 1974.
5. Jensen, Clayne R., *Outdoor Recreation in America*, 3rd ed. Minneapolis: Burgess Publishing Company, 1977.
6. Jensen, Clayne R., and Thornstenson, Clark T. *Issues in Outdoor Recreation*. 2nd ed. Minneapolis: Burgess Publishing Company, 1977.

Chapter 11

IMPACT ON ENVIRONMENTAL EDUCATION

FIFTY YEARS OF RESIDENT OUTDOOR EDUCATION: 1930-1980

by Robert E. Roth, Diane Cantrell,
and Woodward Bousquet

Dr. Robert E. Roth, Ph.D.
Professor and Chairman, Division
   of Environmental Education
School of Natural Resources
The Ohio State University

Diane Cantrell
Teaching associate,
   doctoral student
The Ohio State University

Woodward Bousquet
Teaching associate,
   doctoral student
The Ohio State University

Dr. Robert E. Roth is professor and chairman in the Division of Environmental Education, School of Natural Resources at The Ohio State University where Ms. Diane Cantrell and Mr. Woodward Bousquet are doctoral students and teaching associates.

Dr. Roth was a conservation education supervisor, elementary science teacher, and director of conservation education for the school camp of the Ethical Culture Schools in New York City from 1961-1963. He developed and directed the Lakeside Nature Center in Spring Valley, New York for the Edwin Gould Foundation for Children from 1963-1965 and then was an instructor in the Department of Outdoor Teacher Education, Lorado Taft Field Campus, Northern Illinois University from 1965-67. Following completion of a Ph.D. degree at the University of Wisconsin-Madison in 1969, and after conducting research on environmental education concepts, he joined the faculty of the Division of Environmental Education in the School of Natural Resources at The Ohio State University.

Dr. Roth is a past president of the National Association for Environmental Education and an executive editor of the *Journal of Environmental Education*.

Ms. Diane Cantrell is currently enrolled in a doctoral program though the Department of

Foundations and Research in the College of Education at The Ohio State University. Previous experience includes the teaching of French and English in the Columbus Public Schools from 1971-1975 and serving as an education specialist for the Environmental Education Section of the Ohio Department of Natural Resources. Ms. Cantrell is presently serving as vice president of the Ohio Alliance for Environmental Education and is a past chairperson of the membership committee of that organization. She has served on the board of trustees of the Columbus Audubon Society and is conducting research in the area of environmental education.

Woodward Bousquet is a doctoral student in the Department of Science and Mathematics Education, The Ohio State University. He was formerly the assistant director of the McKeever Environmental Learning Center at Sandy Lake, Pennsylvania, where he worked in staff and student teacher supervision, site and curriculum development, public relations, and the teaching workshops and courses for pre-service and in-service teachers. Mr. Bousquet had previously been employed as an environmental educator in Massachusetts, New York, and New Jersey. He is conducting research in the area of environmental education.

Environmental education, regardless of emphasis or definition, has emerged as an interdisciplinary process with significant historical roots that are intertwined and linked with most resident outdoor education ideas and thrusts. No social movement, educational innovation, or scientific achievement ever occurs in isolation from the ebb and flow of societal concerns.

Accordingly, a number of education-related movements have impacted resident outdoor education resulting in substantial influence on environmental education as well. Of special significance are four intellectual thrusts of the last century, namely: nature study; conservation education and related resource-use education; progressive education; and, science education.(1) Each movement in turn and in concert helped to support, refine, and strengthen a relationship between resident outdoor education and environmental education.

Education-Related Movements

Nature study arose from a growing concern about the inadequacy of 19th century pedagogical techniques that emphasized rote learning, knowledge acquisition primarily through books and lectures, and isolation from real world phenomena and experiences. Louis Agassiz was credited with being the first to verbalize the need to emphasize the study of nature rather than relying entirely on the written and spoken word. Wilbur Jackman, and later Liberty Hyde Bailey, both influenced by Agassiz, provided definition and substance to an educational philosophy that emphasized a holistic approach, encountering the real world at the child's level, and use of all the senses to perceive, feel, and come to know nature.

Conservation education and resource-use education, while arising from concerns about conservation problems related to the misuse of soil, range, forests and wildlife resources, emanated largely from various governmental programs. Such programs significantly influenced the development of resident outdoor education. Approaches to conservation education were deemed important and followed earlier attempts to legislate and enforce conservation laws which did not provide solutions to the problems. A great deal of literature was produced, several laws requiring the teaching of conservation were passed, and resident teacher workshops that provided university credit were established to educate teachers about resource issues, conservation practices, available materials, and teaching activities appropriate for various grade levels. Ohio, for example, established the Conservation Laboratory as a long-term summer resident experience.

The progressive education movement similarly influ-

enced resident outdoor education and the development of environmental education. John Dewey, following Comenius, Rousseau, Pestalozzi, and Froebel encouraged the development of curricular strategies that were responsive to the needs of children and produced curricular reform that has had far-reaching implications. The move toward holistic, interdisciplinary, and real-world approaches, with the well-known dictum, "learn by doing" still interests people today.

Science education benefited from and contributed to the mix of philosophical evolution and educational change as well. From the development of an orderly and scientific process of education conceived by Johann Herbart to the formation of the National Herbartian Society in 1895, (subsequently to be named the National Society for the Study of Education), an orderly assessment of educational thought was instituted that was to guide most educational development from the early 1900s to the present day. Publication of the 1904 National Society for the Scientific Study of Education Yearbook on *Nature Study,*(2) the 1932 yearbook on *A Program for Teaching Science,*(3) and the 1947 yearbook on *Science Education in American Schools,*(4) all marked significant developmental stages in the evolution of science education theory and practice.

School camping in relation to science education became, and continues to be, a major emphasis in many school systems across the United States. Modern day curricular development projects like Biological Sciences Curriculum Study (BSCS), Elementary Science Study (ESS), and Science Curriculum Improvement Study (SCIS) all have components related to land laboratories, school forests, and resident outdoor education settings as part of the experiences suggested for scientific investigation of the natural and human-made worlds.

Evolution of Environmental Education

Resident outdoor education was significantly shaped by these philosophies and educational movements. Environmental education, as influenced by resident outdoor education, also evolved from this rich past. While the term "environmental education" emerged only recently when viewed over time, the related forerunners—nature study education, conservation education, and outdoor education—provided a firm foundation for its development.

Different educators, including Lucas,(5) Donaldson,(6) and Smith,(7) refer to education *in*, *about*, and *for* the environment. Lucas explains that education *in* the environment refers to a teaching method, education *about* the environment concentrates on environmental knowledge, while education *for* the environment empha-

sizes environmental quality. How the contributors to environmental education reflect, in varying degrees, all three of these dimensions will be illustrated in the next section. Such differences serve not only to separate their philosophical positions, but also indicate their contributions to the foundations of environmental education.

Outdoor Education: Education in the Environment

As a teaching method, outdoor education relies on resources outside of the classroom for educational purposes.(8) By providing students with direct learning experiences on the school grounds, in the community, or at nearby natural areas, effective teachers transform the out-of-doors into a working laboratory. Activities draw upon traditional subject areas and enhance the curriculum while immersing children in the environment. Cemetery studies, map and compass exercises, crafts, and creative artistic and written expression represent only a few of the activities teachers employ outdoors to reinforce classroom lessons in math, English, social studies, art, physical education, and health.

While the resources for many of these activities exist nearby or involve only a half- or full-day field trip, the extended school camping experience has become an integral part of many outdoor education programs. Resident outdoor education often culminates a year-long program and adds greater depth and breadth to the knowledge, attitudes, and skills emphasized in the curriculum. In this three- to five-day experience opportunities are provided for social growth, direct learning, skill building, and adventure unmatched in the traditional school setting. Camping, according to L. B. Sharp, plays a very important part in the learning process and "stands at the very peak of outdoor education."(9)

Whether at school or a camp, teaching in the environment helps to meet the aims of education in a way that indoor instruction simply cannot. Similarly, Bernard S. Mason, another tremendous contributor and contemporary of Sharp, in the *Redbook Camp Literature Prize Book* said, "(resident outdoor education) . . . if it is worthy, is one of the greatest socializing, humanizing, civilizing factors which can enter the life of a boy or girl."(10)

Conservation Education and Nature Study: Education about the Environment

While outdoor education is primarily a pedagogic technique, conservation and nature study education, in contrast, draw upon scientific bodies of knowledge.

Conservation education is generally defined as the study of the wise use of natural resources through application of a variety of management practices. This field was spurred by the creation of numerous federal and state conservation agencies and the formation of related private interest groups such as the Izaak Walton League and National Wildlife Federation. Most of these organizations sponsor a wide variety of information and education programs. Agricultural extension offices of colleges and universities, through youth-oriented programs, also provide leadership in conservation education.

In rural schools especially, children study conservation principles and techniques including stream improvement, forest management, soil formation, and farm practices such as contour plowing. Many schools have established conservation education land laboratories on or adjacent to school property to provide actual work experience to complement classroom studies.

Proponents of nature study usually approach education as it relates to the environment in a different manner. Instead of emphasizing human utilization, nature study activities such as tree identification, animal tracking, pond studies, insect rearing, and weather forecasting are designed to give students firsthand understanding and appreciation of the wonders of the natural world. Most studies take place outdoors, but bringing specimens into the classroom for close observation over a longer period of time is also a component of nature study.

Although activities in mathematics, social studies, and language arts are often incorporated into nature study and conservation education programs, investigations of the natural sciences predominate in both fields. The use of the natural environment, a focus upon conservation problems, and the knowledge of natural phenomena have provided significant contributions to the broadly conceived area of environmental education.

Environmental Education: Education in, about, and for the Environment

Beginning in the 1960s, there were indications that a grass roots environmental movement was taking shape. Rachel Carson's *Silent Spring* (1962), Adlai Stevenson's "Spaceship Earth" address to the United Nations (1965), the National Environmental Policy Act (1969), and the first Earth Day (1970) were all landmarks in the evolution of a growing awareness of environmental issues in the minds of American people. Citizens across the nation began to realize that people depend upon and affect the condition of the environment and that, therefore, environmental quality must be maintained and enhanced.

People called upon education to play a major role in facilitating changes in knowledge, beliefs, and lifestyles. It was suggested that not only should some teaching occur outdoors, and school curricula include natural history and resource management techniques, but also that education must provide the environmental concepts, problem-solving skills, and motivation necessary for people to act responsibly to improve environmental quality.

One of the early definitions of environmental education was developed by Dr. Robert Roth in 1969 when he produced and validated a list of 112 concepts appropriate for the field. He stated that the concern of environmental education is to develop citizens that are:

1. knowledgeable about the biophysical and socio-cultural environments of which people are a part;
2. aware of environmental problems and management alternatives of use in solving these problems; and
3. motivated to act responsibly in developing diverse environments that are optimum for living a quality life.(11)

A year later, Congress passed the Environmental Education Act to provide funds for program development and implementation. This legislation included the following description of topics and issues that come under the heading of environmental education:

Environmental education is an integrated process which deals with man's interrelationship with his natural and man-made surroundings, including the relation of population growth, pollution, resource allocation and depletion, conservation, technology, and urban and rural planning to the total human environment. Environmental education is a study of the factors influencing ecosystems, mental and physical growth, living and working conditions, decaying cities, and population pressures. Environmental education is intended to promote among citizens the awareness and understanding of the environment, our relationship to it, and the concern and responsible action necessary to assure our survival and to improve the quality of life.(12)

In 1972 representatives from around the world expressed international concern for environmental quality at the United Nations Conference on the Human Environment in Stockholm. An outgrowth of this meeting was the Belgrade Workshop in 1975, which examined goals and strategies of global environmental education.(13) Following this conceptual phase was the Inter-governmental Conference on Environmental Education, organized by UNESCO and held in Tbilisi, USSR in October, 1977.

The resulting Tbilisi Declaration enumerated recommendations for developing environmental education at the national, regional, and international levels. The following were among the guiding principles identified:

Environmental education is the result of the reorientation and dovetailing of different disciplines and educational experiences which facilitate an integrated perception of the problems of the environment, enabling more rational action, capable of meeting social needs, to be taken.

A basic aim of environmental education is to succeed in making individuals and communities understand the complex nature of the natural and built environments resulting from the interaction of their biological, physical, social, economic and cultural aspects and acquire the knowledge, values, attitudes, and practical skills to participate in a responsible and effective way in anticipating and solving environmental problems, and the management of the quality of the environment.(14)

The three viewpoints outlined have similarities that help explain the scope and approach of environmental education. They indicate that environmental education embraces all disciplines and applies to both formal and nonformal settings. In addition, they characterize environmental education as education *in, about*, and *for* the environment. Education *in* the environment fosters a person's empathy and sense of oneness with his or her surroundings. Education *about* the environment enables people to understand the earth's biophysical and sociocultural environments, and education *for* the environment is designed to generate concern and motivate responsible action.

Environmental education then, is a blending and enhancing of the philosophies of resident outdoor education with those of conservation education, nature study, and various aspects of the environmental movement. What distinguishes environmental education from its forerunners is the incorporation of activities that deal with environmentally responsible behavior. Just as learning experiences are necessary to develop environmental awareness and knowledge, environmental education programs also include specific activities that deal with this crucial third element, behavior. Thus, a close relationship with the historic goals of resident outdoor education continues to be undiminished in an expanded context.

Summary

This year, people all over America will celebrate the fiftieth anniversary of resident outdoor education. Regardless of differences in approach or focus, they will join together in spirit and events to praise the essence of resident outdoor education—its philosophy, structure, techniques, activities, and constancy.

Through the steadfastness of many, resident outdoor education gives strength to each educational field involving the environment. The boundaries blur, the overlap increases, and efforts by one complement efforts by others.

Yet the impact of resident outdoor education is indisputable. It provides a reservoir of environmentally-oriented methods and activities which have been tested and proven successful. These are duplicated or adapted to fit the needs of individual programs. Resident outdoor education and related approaches have become institutionalized through policies, mandates, and legislation. School systems include these different fields in the curriculum by setting specific goals and objectives which

relate to the environment, providing resource materials, developing school sites, and conducting resident outdoor education programs. Federal and state agencies and private organizations now provide a wide range of services to assist in resident education related to the environment and out-of-doors.

As a leading force committed to a quality of life, environmental education stands strong, moving forward, fortified by its past, to shape decisions affecting the future. Sir Issac Newton reflects the position of environmental education today in a line written 300 years ago to scientist Robert Hooke: "If I have seen further (than you and Descartes) it is by standing upon the shoulders of Giants."

Environmental education stands not along, not beside, but upon the shoulders of resident outdoor education.

Northern Illinois University

Selected References

1. Roth, Charles E., "Off the Merry-go-round and on to the Escalator." *From Ought to Action in Environmental Education,* SMEAC Information Reference Center, The Ohio State University, Columbus, 1978.
2. National Society for the Scientific Study of Education, *Nature Study.* Third yearbook, National Society for the Scientific Study of Education, Chicago, 1904.
3. National Society for the Study of Education, *A Program for Teaching Science.* Thirty-first yearbook, National Society for the Study of Education, Chicago, 1947.
4. National Society for the Study of Education, *Science Education in American Schools.* National Society for the Study of Education, Chicago, 1947.
5. Lucas, Arthur M., Environment and Environmental Education: Conceptual Issues and Curriculum Implications. Unpublished doctoral dissertation, The Ohio State University, Columbus, 1972.
6. Donaldson, George W., and Donaldson, Louise E., "Outdoor Education—A Definition." *Journal of Health, Physical Education and Recreation.* 29:17, 63.
7. Smith, Julian W., "The Scope of Outdoor Education." *The Bulletin of the National Association of Secondary School Principals,* 1960. 44: 56-158.
8. Swan, Malcolm., "Forerunners of Environmental Education." McInnis, Noel and Albrecht, Don, *What Makes Education Environmental?* Environmental Educators, Inc., Washington, D.C., and Data Courier, Inc., Louisville, 1975.
9. Sharp, L. B., "What is Outdoor Education?" Hammerman, Donald R., and Hammerman, William M., *Outdoor Education: A Book of Readings.* Burgess Publishing Company, Minneapolis, Minnesota, 1968.
10. Mason, Bernard S., *Camping and Education.* The McCall Company, Publishers, New York, 1930, p. 248.
11. Roth, Robert E., *Fundamental Concepts for Environmental Management Education (K-16).* Unpublished doctoral dissertation, University of Wisconsin, Madison, 1969.
12. U.S. Congress. 1970. The Environmental Education Act of 1970.
13. Stapp, William B. "International Environmental Education: The UNESCO-UNEP Programme." *Journal of Environmental Education.* 1976 8(2):19-25.
14. United Nations Educational, Scientific and Cultural Organization (UNESCO), *Intergovernmental Conference on Environmental Education.* Final Report, United Nations, 1978.

Suggested Readings

Bowman, Mary Lynne and Coon, Herbert L., *Recycling: Activities for the Classroom.* ERIC, Columbus, Ohio: The Ohio State University, 1978.

Bowman, Mary Lynne, Disinger, John F., and Coon, Herbert L., *Land Use Management Activities for the Classroom.* ERIC/SMEAC, Columbus, Ohio: The Ohio State University, 1977.

Coon, Herbert L., and Alexander, Michele Y., *Energy Activities for the Classroom.* ERIC, Columbus, Ohio: The Ohio State University, 1976.

Coon, Herbert L., and Bowman, Mary Lynne, *Environmental Education in the Urban Setting: Rationale and Teaching Activities.* ERIC, Columbus, Ohio: The Ohio State University, 1976.

Hernbrode, William R., *Multidisciplinary Wildlife Teaching Activities.* ERIC, Columbus, Ohio: The Ohio State University, 1978.

McInnis, Noel, and Albrecht, Don, *What Makes Education Environmental?* Washington: Environmental Educators, Inc., 1975.

Roth, Robert E., *A Review of Research Related to Environmental Education,* 1973-1976. ERIC/SMEAC, Columbus, Ohio: The Ohio State University, 1976.

Schultz, Judith M., *Population Education Activities for the Classroom,* ERIC, Columbus, Ohio: The Ohio State University, 1977.

Simon, Sidney B., Howe, Leland W. and Kirschenbaum, Howard, *Values Clarification; a Handbook of Practical Strategies for Teachers and Students.* New York: Hart Publishing Company, 1972.

Stapp, William B., (ed.) *From Ought to Action in Environmental Education.* Conference report of The Alliance for Environmental Education, SMEAC Information Reference Center, Columbus, Ohio, 1978.

Swan, James, and Stapp, William B., *Environmental Education: Strategies Toward a More Livable Future.* New York: SAGE Publications, John Wiley & Sons, 1974.

Terry, Mark, *Teaching for Survival.* New York: Ballantine Books, Inc., 1971.

Troost, C. J., and Altman, H., *Environmental Education—A Sourcebook.* New York: John Wiley & Sons, 1972.

Van Matre, Steve, *Sunship Earth.* Martinsville, Indiana: American Camping Association, 1979.

Wheatley, John H., and Coon, Herbert L., *Teaching Activities in Environmental Education—Volume II.* ERIC, Columbus, Ohio. The Ohio State University, 1974.

Wheatley, John H., and Coon, Herbert L., *Teaching Activities in Environmental Education—Volume III.* ERIC, Columbus, Ohio: The Ohio State University, 1975.

Chapter 12

IMPACT ON TEACHER EDUCATION
FIFTY YEARS OF RESIDENT OUTDOOR EDUCATION: 1930-1980

by Donald R. Hammerman

Donald R. Hammerman, Ed.D.
Professor of Outdoor Teacher Education
Lorado Taft Field Campus
Northern Illinois University

Donald R. Hammerman's career includes teaching sixth grade in Maryland, working at the Battle Creek Outdoor Education Center at Clear Lake Camp in Michigan, and a combination of teaching and adminstration at Northern Illinois University. For twelve years Dr. Hammerman served as chairperson, Department of Outdoor Teacher Education, and has been director of the Taft Campus from 1965-1979.

During more than a quarter century of direct involvement in outdoor education, Dr. Hammerman has co-authored two books: *Teaching in the Outdoors* and *Outdoor Education: A Book of Readings*, both in their second edition. He has written four film scripts and numerous articles for various professional journals. He has led three foreign study tours to examine programs of outdoor education in Europe.

Dr. Hammerman is a past chairperson of the Council on Outdoor Education, has served on the Advisory Board for ERIC/CRESS, on the Editorial Board of the *Journal of Health, Physical Education, Recreation*, and as contributing editor to *The Communicator*. He has appeared as keynote speaker, panelist, and moderator at various national conventions and regional and state conferences. He was selected as one of two special resource leaders from the U.S. to serve in an advisory capacity to the Canadian Camping Association National Conference on Outdoor Education at St. Agathe, Canada, 1974. Dr. Hammerman was the 1966 recipient of the Howard Bell Award for outstanding contributions to outdoor education.

Developments that affect societal institutions rarely occur in a vacuum. Institutions of higher education, sooner or later, reflect the elements of change that are impacting the schools. Early in the history of outdoor education a few select teacher education institutions recognized first, the need to provide training in ways of utilizing out-of-classroom environments for instructional purposes and second, the opportunity to capitalize on an innovative curriculum development. Institutions of higher education are not often in the vanguard of a new movement; such was the case with resident outdoor education. While resident outdoor education had its formalized beginnings on an experimental basis in the United States, mainly during the thirties, a decade passed before a limited number of teachers colleges began to sponsor conferences and offer workshops and institutes focusing on educational programs dealing with what, at the time, was termed "camping education."

Early Teacher Education Programs

One of the earliest teacher education developments was a cooperative effort between New York State Teachers Colleges and L. B. Sharp's National Camp. A ten day Camping Education Institute was held at National Camp, Life Camps in Sussex, New Jersey in 1941. The institute was repeated in 1942 and included faculty and student representatives from state teachers colleges in New Jersey as well as New York. The following year several Pennsylvania State Teachers Colleges joined the institute.

Some colleges established their own resident outdoor centers. In the mid-forties the State Teachers Colleges at Fredonia, Plattsburg and Cortland, New York located sites and developed programs. These campuses are now part of the State University system. The New Jersey School of Conservation situated in Stokes State Forest has been offering a variety of teacher education programs since 1949. Antioch College, Yellow Springs, Ohio has had a long-standing involvement with outdoor education, offering a broad program of experiences at the Glen Helen Nature Center. Other institutions that developed branch campuses or field campuses in the early fifties for the purpose of providing teacher education experiences outdoors include: Boston University, Indiana University, New York University, Northern Illinois University, and Southern Illinois University.

A number of institutions have gone another route and provide pre-service and in-service teachers with opportunities to engage in organized internships at various outdoor education centers throughout the U.S. At least one university (Northern Illinois University) also offers internships at selected outdoor education centers in Canada, England, Scotland and Germany.

National Conferences

In September, 1949 the first National Conference on Community School Camping was held at Haven Hill Lodge in Michigan.(1) In attendance were national leaders in government, conservation and education, as well as representatives from organizations and agencies having a special interest in school camping (resident outdoor education). The need to prepare teachers to assume active roles of leadership in resident outdoor centers (school camps) was recognized and the conference membership recommended among other things, that, " . . . general programs for all teachers in training including camping experience (be implemented) to insure understanding and cooperation in camping programs." Three college presidents participated in this milestone conference. A few years later, as a direct result of this conference, rather extensive program developments in outdoor education were implemented at Northern Illinois University and Southern Illinois University.

A national workshop held at Clear Lake Camp, Dowling, Michigan, in June, 1953, attracted a select group of seventy-eight teacher educators primarily from eastern, southeastern and midwestern states. Sixteen teacher training institutions were represented. This conference, sponsored by the Michigan Department of Public Instruction and subsidized by the Kellogg Foundation, utilized a workshop approach over a week-long period. The workshop format permitted participants to engage in prolonged and intensive discussion centering around outdoor education and school camping in teacher training programs.

The Midwest Outdoor Education Conference held at Southern Illinois University in Carbondale, March 18-19, 1960, attracted a distinguished group of teacher educators, who gathered to assess the current status of outdoor education, and to plot future directions in higher education. This gathering laid the groundwork for the First National Conference on the Preparation of Teachers which was to follow in September, 1960 at Northern Illinois University. Much time was devoted to a discussion of teacher needs and how to help teachers develop the capabilities required to take children into the schoolyard, or on extended day trips, or travel-study experiences, or into the school camp setting. Conferees felt rather strongly that at least part of the teacher education program should take place in the out-of-doors itself in order to encourage more teachers to conduct a variety of educational experiences beyond the classroom.

A meeting billed as the "First National Conference on the Preparation of Teachers for Carrying Suitable Portions of the Curriculum to the Out-of-Doors," was held at NIU's Lorado Taft Field Campus, Oregon, Illinois, in September, 1960. This conference attracted educators from fourteen different teacher preparation institutions ranging from New Jersey in the East to Iowa in the Mid-West. Conference participants engaged in discussion and debate as they pondered: (a) the values to be attained through outdoor education, (b) how to build an outdoor education philosophy in a college or university staff, (c) the impact of outdoor education upon the public school, its curriculum, and its teachers and (d) the use of resource people in the program.

Lawrence H. Conrad, Editor of the *Conference Proceedings*, in "The Findings of the Conference, Preliminary Statement," wrote: "The prime goal of Outdoor Teacher Education should be to develop an awareness and an understanding of the natural environment in its relationship to all knowledge. This should surely be a part of every teacher's professional preparation, both for indoor and outdoor teaching. By the time the goal has been reached in the professional colleges across the country, our educational system will have undergone wide reorganization, and our schools and colleges will be enriched and improved."(3)

Growth of Programs in Higher Education

The impact of outdoor education on programs of teacher education is dramatically reflected in a compilation of outdoor education degree programs completed for ERIC/CRESS in 1977 by Russel E. Bachert, Jr., entitled, *Directory of Outdoor Education Degree Programs in Higher Education*. Bachert found sixty colleges and universities in thirty-one states offering degree programs at the undergraduate and graduate level. These programs were labeled according to a variety of terms: "Environmental Education," "Outdoor Education," "Environmental Interpretation," "Outdoor Education/Recreation," and "Interpretation." Other programs were identified as "Areas of Concentration," "Areas of Emphasis," or "Areas" of Specialization."(2)

Bachert's survey revealed that an increasing number of colleges and universities have acquired and developed their own permanent sites as resident outdoor/environmental education centers, or are utilizing other sites and facilities, not owned by the institution, for this purpose. The following institutions indicated they have their own field campus, or other comparable outdoor environmental study area:

1. Arizona State University
2. California State University at Hayward
3. Humbolt State University, California
4. San Francisco State University, California
5. Colorado State University
6. University of Northern Colorado
7. University of Western Florida
8. University of Idaho
9. George Williams College, Illinois
10. Northern Illinois University
11. Southern Illinois University
12. Western Illinois University
13. Ball State University, Indiana
14. Indiana University
15. Eastern Kentucky University
16. Western Kentucky University
17. University of Maine at Orono
18. Catonsville Community College, Maryland
19. University of Maryland
20. Northeastern University, Illinois
21. Michigan State University
22. Bemidji State University, Minnesota
23. Central Missouri State University
24. University of Nebraska at Omaha
25. Antioch—New Hampshire, Ohio
26. Glassboro State College, New Jersey
27. Monclair State College, New Jersey
28. Cornell University, New York
29. State University at Cortland, New York
30. State University College at New Paltz, New York
31. State University College at Plattsburg, New York
32. State University of New York, Syracuse
33. Appalacian State University, North Carolina
34. University of North Carolina at Greensboro
35. The Ohio State University at Columbus
36. The Ohio State University, Newark Campus
37. Oklahoma State University
38. Southwestern Oklahoma State University
39. Southern Oregon State College
40. University of Oregon
41. California State College, Pennsylvania
42. Kutztown State College, Pennsylvania
43. Mercyhurst College, Pennsylvania
44. The Pennsylvania State University
45. Slippery Rock College, Pennsylvania
46. Temple University, Pennsylvania
47. The University of Tennessee at Martin
48. Texas A & M University
49. Johnson State College, Vermont
50. University of Washington
51. University of Wisconsin, Stevens Point

© Phiz Mezey

Experimentation—Research

Most educational innovations ultimately lead to a spate of formalized research at the graduate level. Outdoor education has been no exception. Very early in the formative years of resident outdoor education (initially referred to as camping education and later school camping), doctoral studies were conducted to assess the status of outdoor education in teaching in the public schools and in teacher education institutions.(24) Two decades later Diane Pick followed up with an assessment of current status and recommendations for the future of college and university outdoor education centers.(22)

College courses in camping education were being developed and offered to both prospective and in-service teachers.(18) Plans were formulated for developing leadership competencies in school camping and outdoor education for elementary education students, and competencies needed by classroom teachers in resident outdoor programs were identified. (12, 17)

Proposals for incorporating outdoor education as an integral part of teacher preparation were developed and evaluative studies carried out by Rhead(23), Kalla(19), and Weiss(26). Several studies developed plans for administering various college and university camps and resident outdoor education programs.(11, 20, 21, 25)

Teacher education was scrutinzed to determine the kinds of outdoor education experiences that were significant for elementary teachers(13), the effects of learning outdoors on teaching behavior in the classroom(16), and the impact of resident outdoor education on elementary education majors' understanding of how learning is facilitated.(14)

Concluding Statement

Resident outdoor education has literally introduced a breath of fresh air to some rather stagnant programs of teacher preparation. Pre-service teachers whose contact with children has been limited to a formal classroom situation have been provided the opportunity to live with youngsters and assume responsibility for their learning and their welfare in the total-living atmosphere of a resident outdoor center. In this setting, future teachers are thrust into situations where they learn to confront children in out-of-classroom environments. They are able to observe youngsters in a more natural behavioral setting—with the result that lessons of the psychology text take on more valid and more realistic meaning. The impact of resident outdoor education on teacher education, while not comprehensive, has been intensive in those institutions where it has been implemented. The hundreds of courses and programs available to pre-service and in-service teachers is evidence of the profound influence that outdoor education has had and is presently exerting on teacher education in the United States.

Selected References

1. "A Report of the National Conference on Community School Camping," Department of Public Instruction, Lansing, Michigan, 1949.
2. Bachert, Russell E. Jr. *Directory of Outdoor Education Degree Programs in Higher Education,* Austin, Texas: National Educational Laboratory Publishers, Inc., 1977.
3. Conrad, Lawrence H. "Outdoor Teacher Education: A Report Drawn from the First National Conference on the Preparation of Teachers for Carrying Suitable Portions of the Curriculum to the Out-of-Doors," Northern Illinois University, DeKalb, Illinois, 1961.
4. Cross, Carole B. "A Study of the Development of Clear Lake Camp," Unpublished master's thesis, Northern Illinois University, 1967.
5. *Extending Education,* Outdoor Education Association, Inc. August, 1960, 5:11, pp. 1-8.
6. Hammerman, Donald R. and William M. *Outdoor Education: A Book of Readings*, Minneapolis, Minnesota: Burgess Publishing Co., 1973.
7. Smith, Carlson, Donaldson, Masters, *Outdoor Education,* Englewood Cliffs, New Jersey: Prentice-Hall, Inc., 1965.
8. Smith, Julian W. et al, *Outdoor Education for American Youth,* American Alliance Health. Physical Education, Recreation, Washington, D.C. 1957.
9. Swan, Hammerman, Stark, "Dissertations in ECO Education," Taft Campus Occasional Paper #15, Lorado Taft Field Campus, Northern Illinois University, Oregon, Illinois 1976.
10. Swan, Stark, Hammerman, *Research in Outdoor Education: Summaries of Doctoral Studies,* Washington, D.C.: Council on Outdoor Education, Association of the American Alliance for Health, Physical Education and Recreation, 1978.

Doctoral Dissertations

11. Archard, Merrill, *Recommendations for the Administration of the New Palz State Teachers College School Camp,* New York University, 1956.
12. Berger, Harriet, *A Plan for Developing Competencies for Leadership in School Camping and Outdoor Education for Elementary Education Students,* New York University, 1958.
13. Cyphers, Vincent, *A Study to Determine the Significant Outdoor Experiences for Elementary Teachers,* Colorado State University, 1961.
14. Hammerman, William. *An Investigation of the Effect of an Outdoor Education Experience Upon Elementary Education Students' Understanding of How Learning is Facilitated.* University of Maryland, 1958.
15. Hartung, John. *An Evaluation of an Experimental Stress—Challenge Environmental Education College Course.* Southern Illinois University, 1973.
16. Hauserman, Billy. *The Effect of an Orientation to the Outdoors on Teaching Behavior in the Classroom.* SUNY at Buffalo, 1963.
17. Holt, Lillabelle. *Identification of the Competencies Needed by the Classroom Teacher in Programs of Resident Outdoor Education.* Ohio University, 1973.
18. Irwin, Frank. *Camping Education—Outline for College Course in Camping Education.* New York University, 1948.
19. Kalla, Joseph. *An Evaluation of an Interdisciplinary Program in an Elementary Teacher-Education Curriculum.* University of Wyoming, 1972.
20. Lantz, Everett. *A Prospectus for the Administration of College and University Camps.* University of California, 1955.
21. McCall, Margaret Ann. *The Organization and Administration of Camps Conducted by Departments of Physical Education in Colleges, Teacher Training Institutions and Universities in the U.S.* New York University, 1943.
22. Pick, Diane. *College and University Outdoor Education Centers—Present Status and Recommendations for the Future.* Indiana University, 1972.
23. Rhead, Raymond. *A Proposed Interdisciplinary Approach to an Outdoor Education Program in the Professional Teacher Preparation Curriculum at Weber State College.* University of Utah, 1967.
24. Shelar, Eugene. *A Study of the Use That is Being Made of the Out-of-Doors in Teaching in the Public Schools and in the Teacher Training Schools.* Cornell University, 1949.
25. Turner, Walton. *Analysis to Determine Significant Administrative Procedures Used in the Establishment and Operation of Selected Resident Outdoor Laboratory School Programs.* Colorado State University, 1967.
26. Weiss, Iris. *The Development and Evaluation of a Self-Investigational Environmental Education Program for Teachers.* University of North Carolina, 1974.

© Donald Rettew

Chapter 13

IMPACT ON HIGHER EDUCATION
FIFTY YEARS OF RESIDENT OUTDOOR EDUCATION: 1930-1980

by Russel E. Bachert, Jr.

Russel E. Bachert, Jr., Ed.D.
Assistant Professor of Outdoor/
    Environmental Education
Director, Piney Lake Field Campus
University of North Carolina at Greensboro

Russel E. Bachert, Jr., has been active in the field of outdoor education for more than fifteen years as an elementary classroom teacher, resident outdoor education teacher, camp director, and university professor. Earlier camp counseling positions led to his employment at the Battle Creek Outdoor Education Center in Michigan, the Newfound Harbor Marine Institute in Florida, and the National Wildlife Federation as summer director of their Wildlife Camp and Environmental Adventures program in North Carolina.

Dr. Bachert was the 1974-75 recipient of the Conservation Fellowship Award given by the National Wildlife Federation and Indiana University's Lebert H. Weir Award in 1975. He has participated in numerous courses in camping and outdoor education sponsored by the National Outdoor Leadership School, the Red Ridge College of River Canoeing, the Audubon Society, the American Youth Hostel's Leadership Training School, the American Camping Association, the American Red Cross, and the North Carolina Outward Bound School.

Dr. Bachert was instrumental in organizing the North Carolina Outdoor Education Association and lists among his publications: *Outdoor Education Equipment: Plans for Easy-to-Make Items; Eco-Sketch: Ideas for Environmental Education; Directory of Outdoor Education Degree Programs in Higher Education;* and *Outdoor/Environmental Education Handbook.* He has been president of the Environmental and Outdoor Education Materials, Co., and the owner/director of a private camp that promotes environmental education through adventure. His major effort over the past few years has been the development of an environmental, camping and outdoor education program at the University of North Carolina at Greensboro.

The growth of "modern" outdoor education is reflected in America's institutions of higher education. As the outdoor education movement spread across our land from 1930 to 1980, its philosophy was shaped, its foundation was firmly grounded in sound educational theory and practice, and its acceptance as an important change agent in our educational systems grew. New ideas need time to take hold and be accepted. The need for formal training of leadership in institutions of higher education came slowly, awaiting the appropriate maturation of this phenomena.

Long before any need was created for formal degree programs to train leaders in the field of outdoor education, there came a string of significant individuals and events. Men like L. B. Sharp, Julian W. Smith, William G. Vinal, George W. Donaldson, and Harlan G. Metcalf set the stage by acting as spokesmen and catalysts, breathing life into the ideas embodied by outdoor education. Because of their dynamic leadership qualities and the soundness of the philosophy of outdoor education they and others like them spread the word through lectures, conferences, workshops, articles, books, and leadership training programs.

Leadership training was seen as an effective way to reach more people and affect more lives with the inherent multiplier effect in this approach. These early training programs were usually informal in nature and consisted of short-term workshops and institutes. Perhaps the best known of these was National Camp started by L. B. Sharp in 1940. He brought together selected leaders and students from across the country to share and learn together in a camp setting. University credit was made available for each of these ten-day institutes in outdoor education held in the summers. Obviously, the more leaders trained, the greater the likelihood that the number and size of America's outdoor education programs would grow.

As the outdoor education movement matured and more public schools, organized camps, parks, recreation departments, and government agencies embraced the need for outdoor education programs, a greater impetus existed for establishing formalized degree programs in institutions of higher education. Creation of these degree programs would, with time, put the field of outdoor education on a higher educational and professional plane by providing better quality and more intensified educational training. Little or no research had been done on the impact of outdoor education on higher education until 1970, when the author endeavored to conduct an initial study.

The result of that effort was a nationwide survey that attempted to discover and describe degree programs related to outdoor education. The study was sponsored and endorsed by the Conservation Education Association, the Committee on Professional Preparation of the Council on Outdoor Education, and the Outdoor Education Project of the American Association for Health, Physical Education, and Recreation. Data gathered was later published as the *Directory of Degree Programs Related to Conservation, Ecology, Environmental Education, Environmental Science, Outdoor Education and Natural Resources.*

In early 1976, the author was asked by the Educational Resources Information Center Clearinghouse on Rural Education and Small Schools (ERIC/CRESS), the government clearinghouse on outdoor education in New Mexico, to conduct an up-to-date analysis of outdoor education degree programs in higher education. This was a more extensive and intensive survey than the initial study done in 1970, and it provided the information for what eventually culminated in the *Directory of Outdoor Education Degree Programs in Higher Education* published in June 1977.(1) Dr. Everett D. Edington, director of the Center stated at that time:

> The purpose of this document is to develop a listing and description of outdoor education programs in institutions of higher education, with an emphasis on training educational personnel. The proposed audience is prospective students, outdoor educators, and employers.

This publication provides the substance for the generalizations that are drawn about the impact of outdoor education on higher education. It should be kept in mind that the *Directory* was originally intended to list and describe these degree programs in a very general manner. It was never intended to provide statistical data from which to draw inferences and conclusions. Often those institutions responding to the data gathering instrument and the request for specific information failed to provide any answers or presented them in such an irregular manner as to exclude them from consideration in the analysis to be presented.

The *Directory* represents a compilation of institutions of higher education in the United States that offer a degree program and/or a concentration within a degree program in any of the following areas: outdoor education, environmental education, conservation education and/or environmental interpretation. Each institutional entry includes the following information: name of institution, contact person with mailing address and phone, academic location, degree(s) offered in field, number of full-time and part-time faculty, with a description of their degrees and rank, founding date of department and degree program(s), credit hour requirements, course titles and descriptions, number of students enrolled in and graduated from each program offered, approximate number of total students enrolled in various degree programs and percentage of those in outdoor education program(s), forecast of future developments in outdoor education within the institution, and a description of any field campus or outdoor education center used in conjunction with the outdoor education degree program(s).

From the more than 275 letters of invitation and survey forms sent to gather information for the *Directory,* ninety-five completed responses were received. Of that number, sixty-four academic divisions located within sixty different colleges and universities located in thirty-one states qualified for inclusion. One university, Michigan State, offered degree programs in four entirely different academic divisions. Although every effort was made to discover all programs that existed in the United States, certainly some eluded the study. The degree programs offered by these institutions mirror the historical evolution of outdoor education over these past fifty years of growth and development. Each one has a story to tell about who started it, why it is located where it is—geographically and academically, the name it was given, the types of courses it offers, and all of the other unique characteristics it encompasses.

Of those sixty-four academic divisions offering outdoor education degree programs, they can be clustered according to geographic areas of the country as follows:

Geographic Area	Number in Area
Mid-Atlantic	17
Midwest	17
West	10
South	8
New England	6
Southwest	3

The particular location of a program(s) in one state or area of the country is likely tied to one or more of these historical developments. *(a)* home base of an early and/or present day leader(s) in the field; *(b)* bastion of resident outdoor education in the public schools; *(c)* state department(s) provided strong direction and impetus in outdoor education; and/or *(d)* the location of an effective state or regional outdoor education organization(s).

Historically, the first institution in the *Directory* listed as having a degree program in the field was Cornell University with a beginning date of 1888. This program was obviously connected with Liberty Hyde Bailey and the nature study movement, a precursor to the outdoor education movement. The next program noted falls within the

beginning years of the "modern" outdoor education era. In 1937 a program in nature recreation was established by Cap'n Bill Vinal, an early leader in the field, at the University of Massachusetts. The year 1946 saw two programs initiated in the field, one at Indiana University and the other at the Pennsylvania State University. In 1947 the University of Wisconsin—Stevens Point started a degree in conservation education while the following year, a program in nature recreation and interpretation began at the State University of New York College at Cortland. Thus, one program began in the 1930s and three in the decade of the 1940s. It is interesting to note that of the four programs developed in the era of "modern" outdoor education, three were offered within the field of recreation, while one was in the sciences and none were in education.

Northern Illinois University

It was not until 1953 that another program came into being, and between the years of 1953 and 1963 five more degree programs in outdoor education began: Michigan State University, College of Education (1953); University of Northern Colorado (1958); Michigan State University, College of Agriculture and Natural Resources (1960); University of Oregon (1961); and Northern Illinois University (1962). The years between 1963 and 1970 saw the emergence of sixteen programs, while 1970 to 1977 marked the beginning of thirty-six programs. There were a multitude of factors that precipitated the growth pattern outlined here, but it would be impossible to list them all since they evolved from a complex pattern of socio-economic-cultural forces. However, it is certain that some of these forces carried greater impact than others and can be singled out because of their greater historical visibility and documentation.

The slow process of building a receptivity for the need and acceptance of degree programs in higher education might better be understood if we look back and study the history of outdoor education in America. Although one cannot begin to catalog all of the significant events that set the stage for the state of outdoor education in higher education as we now know it, certain events can be isolated. Some red-letter dates in the history of outdoor education that probably were most influential in precipitating, indirectly, the development of these degree programs have been selected.

Year	Event
1925	Start of Life Camps
1930	Publication of L. B. Sharp's dissertation
1940	Establishment of National Camp
1940	Initiation of the Clear Lake Camp School Camping Experiment
1949	National Conference on Community School Camping
1955	Beginning of the American Association of Health, Physical Education, and Recreation's Outdoor Education Project
1965	Passage of the Elementary and Secondary Education Act by Congress
1970	First Earth Day
1970	Passage of the Environmental Education Act by Congress

The degrees available in outdoor education are of a diverse nature, ranging from an endorsement to a doctorate in the field. A total of approximately 108 combinations of degrees were listed in the *Directory*. The

breakdown of these degrees according to the number available at various levels is as follows:

Level of Degree	Number of Degrees
Associate	2
Bachelor's	43
Master's	44
Specialist	5
Doctorate	16

Some of these degrees are offered in the field, while others represent concentrated course work within the framework of another degree. Many institutions offer several possible combinations for earning degrees. The University of Northern Colorado provides a student with nine different options for earning a degree in outdoor education, ranging from a bachelor's to a doctoral degree. The highest incidence of these degrees occurs within three areas: recreation, education, and the sciences. Since there are at least twenty-eight unique ways to categorize and name these degrees, the figures stated below are only approximations. Of the 108 combinations of degrees, those with any frequency of occurance are listed:

Academic Specialization	Number of Degrees
Recreation	37
Education	13
Elementary Education	7
Curriculum	7
Interdisciplinary	7
Natural Resources	7

To illustrate the diversity in the types of degrees, now offered in outdoor education, several were selected from the *Directory* and are presented here:

A.A. in Recreation and Parks (Option in Outdoor Education)
B.S. in Health, Leisure, and Sports (Concentration in Environmental Education)
B.S. in Natural Resources (Concentration in Natural Resources Interpretation)
M.A. in Outdoor Education and Conservation
M.A. in Education (Concentration in ECO Education—Environmental, Camping, and/or Outdoor Education)
Ed.S., Specialist in Education in Outdoor-Environmental Education
Ph.D. in Environmental Education

To minimize confusion and maximize consistency, the author has consistently used the term outdoor education when referring to degree programs. As can be noted above, there is little apparent agreement among those in the field as to the term or terms that should be used to name and describe it. The terminology used in identifying these degrees reveals the historical evolution of outdoor education and the numerous rubrics attached to it through time. The field of outdoor education has been ladened with names in attempts to define and redefine it. How adequately they apply to what they name is entirely dependent upon the perception of the individual(s) responsible for titling the degree(s). An analysis of the terminology reveals the use of twenty-eight different descriptors among the 108 degree programs. Of those descriptions, twenty-two were used only once, and the other six terms were used more frequently as shown below:

Terminology	Frequency of Use
Environmental Education	20
Outdoor Education	11
Environmental Interpretation	10
Outdoor/Environmental Education	5
Outdoor Recreation/Education	3
Outdoor Education/Recreation	3

Because of the many connotations and philosophical concepts attached to each of these terms and the fact that there is little agreement among the professionals in

© Laura Huff

the field as to the "best" name, standardization of terminology may never occur.

The number of courses offered and required for individual degree programs differ from institution to institution. They range from several colleges and universities that had only one specialized course in outdoor education and relied heavily on related course work in other departments to one institution, George Williams College, that offered twenty-six specialized courses within their department. Courses offered within any degree program can usually be grouped around six basic areas of emphasis. These areas of emphasis follow with an example of a course that one of the institutions, from the *Directory*, included as part of their course work in outdoor education:

1. Natural History—"Field Natural History for Teachers"
2. Historical and Philosophical Foundations of Outdoor Education—"Environmental Education and the Concept of Values"
3. Recreational Skills—"Outdoor Challenge/Adventure Education"
4. Interpretive Teaching Techniques—"Interpretive Exhibit Preparation"
5. Field Experiences in Outdoor Education—"Resident Outdoor Education Participation"
6. Administration—"Interpretation and Management of Historic Areas"

The uniqueness of these curricula is contained in their course offerings. Many of the courses listed at a college or university can be found at no other, such as: "Environmental and Natural History Writing," "Teaching the Age of Homespun," and "Outdoor Education Short Course—God and His Great Outdoors."

Gathering data to accurately gauge the number of students who have graduated or will graduate with degrees in outdoor education is difficult. Some colleges and universities indicate they do not have past records and make no attempt to keep any at present. It is for this reason that the figures presented here are, at best, a rough approximation based upon the tabular data the author was able to extract from the *Directory*.

Level of Degree	Number Graduated	Number Enrolled—1977
Associate	36	36
Bachelor's	1,243	2,733
Master's	1,323	1,154
Specialist	6	28
Doctorate	27	23
Total	2,635	3,974

Between 1930 and 1976, approximately 2,635 students graduated with degrees in outdoor education. Those students now enrolled, who are expected to graduate in the near future, number about 3,974. It is estimated that the average percentage of students working toward outdoor education degrees within an academic department/division at any of the institutions offering these degrees is approximately 22.2 percent of the student body enrolled in that particular department/divisions.

The background of the faculty who teach outdoor education courses and direct students in these degree programs are as varied as the degrees themselves. Distinct patterns were difficult to discern. Only a few faculty members actually held a professional degree in outdoor education. This can be accounted for since most degree programs in the field have evolved only within the last thirteen years. The number of faculty employed to teach in outdoor education ranged from only one part-time position to as many as ten full-time and six part-time faculty positions in one department.

Thirty-three colleges and universities indicated they owned their own field campuses designed specifically for outdoor education. Ten used other properties owned by their institution, and fifteen mentioned use of facilities and properties not owned by their institution. Thus fifty-eight out of sixty institutions considered ownership and/or availability of outdoor laboratories as vital to the quality of the instruction and experiences provided to the students in their outdoor education degree program(s).

Characterizing the outdoor education field campuses, owned by the institutions themselves, are a wide variety of natural and man-made features: lakes, forests, fields, large tracts of adjacent public land, dormitories, cabins, kitchens, dining halls, resource centers, offices, and shelters. Some of these field campuses are located as close as the main campus itself, and others are one hundred or more miles away. Where the college or university did not own a facility specifically designed for outdoor education, often other facilities owned by their institution were used—such as a fish hatchery, oceanographic institute, school forest, wildlife preserve, or a geology field camp. When the institution did not own an appropriate facility or property, alternatives were sought for outdoor education laboratory experiences. These included a battlefield, a fort, a Boy Scout reservation, a YMCA camp, a state conservation school, a cemetary, and a parking lot.

The institutions responding to the initial study were asked to project developments they anticipated in regard to their outdoor education degree program(s).

Those developments are as follows and range, in order, from those most, to those least frequently mentioned:

Frequency of Mention	Projected Future Developments
13	Create greater interdepartmental cooperation within the institution
11	Expand and improve field experience opportunities for students in outdoor education
9	Start an outdoor education field campus
8	Offer more extension and outreach programs to schools and community groups in outdoor education
7	Expand outdoor education course offerings
6	Expand present outdoor education field campus operation
5	Initiate a master's degree program in outdoor education
4	Add additional faculty in outdoor education
4	Establish a consortium with environmental agencies and community groups
3	Offer new degree options in outdoor education within existing degree programs
3	Place more emphasis on research in outdoor education
3	Upgrade and strengthen outdoor education course offerings
3	Initiate a bachelor's degree program in outdoor education
3	Write grants to secure additional staff, facilities, and equipment

The above responses may foretell possible trends in the continuing impact of outdoor education on higher education in America.

In retrospect, outdoor education has had a tremendous impact on higher education in America during the fifty-year period, 1930 to 1980. Some of these effects, such as the increase in the number of degrees being offered, are more discernable than others. Vestiges of the early roots of the outdoor education movement in school camping can be seen in some of the courses now being offered at several institutions: "School Camping," "School Camping and Outdoor Recreation," and "Resident Outdoor Education Participation." Generalizations about this impact can give a broad overview in an attempt to clarify a complex and multifaceted phenomenon. A careful study of these past developments may help us to more carefully monitor and guide the future of outdoor education. Based on the author's study, the following generalizations about the impact of outdoor education on higher education in America are offered.

1. Development of outdoor education degree programs parallels the historical evolution of the field.
2. A strong relationship exists between the development of outdoor education in the public schools and in higher education.
3. An acknowledged need exists for students in outdoor education degree programs to get extensive practical experience.
4. Value is placed on providing training for students in outdoor education degree programs in natural environments.
5. The diversity and the lack of standardization of terminology in the field reflects divergent philosophical viewpoints of its leaders.
6. Agreement with certain basic philosophical tenets among professional educators in outdoor education is evident when the structure of outdoor education degree programs is examined.
7. The number of degree programs offered in outdoor education is most strongly rooted in the fields of recreation, education, and the sciences—in that order.
8. More degree programs in outdoor education exist within the field of recreation because its historical development parallels that of outdoor education and because many of the early leaders in both of these fields were one and the same person.
9. A strong relationship exists between the historical development of outdoor education in organized camping and in higher education.
10. Professional training of leaders in outdoor education through degree programs in the field, is seen as a way to upgrade the profession and to extend and project the need for outdoor education as an integral part of America's educational system.

We have just taken a look back at the impact of outdoor education on higher education in America and we must now look to the future. Such a young and dynamic phenomenon as the growth and development of outdoor education degree programs needs and deserves more study. Since so little research has been attempted, there is much information and data that should be generated to guide future decisions. The author would like to suggest these topics as needing research now—and in the next fifty years:

1. Study the historical development and impact of the earlier outdoor education degree programs.
2. Study the societal, economic, and cultural influences that affected the growth and development of outdoor education degree programs.
3. Gather more accurate data on the number of students who have graduated and are expected to graduate with outdoor education degrees.
4. Analyze the unique characteristics embodied by particular outdoor education degree programs and the reasons for students electing to earn them.
5. Investigate the local, state, national, and/or international effects a particular institution of higher education has had on the field of outdoor education.
6. Gather data on the present and projected number and types of job placements opportunities for graduates of outdoor education degree programs.

Outdoor education has made its mark on America's institutions of higher education. The proliferation of outdoor education degree programs is an indication that outdoor education is alive and growing. We must now stop and examine the reasons for past growth and the need for future growth and change. These past fifty years of outdoor education have prepared the way for at least another fifty!

Selected References

1. Bachert, Russel E., Jr., *Directory of Degree Programs Related to Conservation, Ecology, Environmental Science, Environmental Education and Natural Resources.* Danville, Illinois. Interstate Printers and Publishers, Inc., 1970.
2. Bachert, Russel E., Jr., *Directory of Outdoor Education Degree Programs in Higher Education.* Austin, Texas: National Educational Laboratory Publishers, Inc., 1977.
3. Bachert, Russel E., Jr., "Status of Outdoor Education Degree Programs." *Journal of Physical Education and Recreation,* January, 1978.
4. Hammerman, Donald R., and William M. *Outdoor Education: A Book of Readings.* 2d. ed. Minneapolis: Burgess Publishing Co., 1973.
5. Rillo, Thomas J. "Historical Background and Development of Camping and Outdoor Education." Mimeographed, n.d.
6. Smith, Julian W., et. al. *Outdoor Education.* 2d. ed. Englewood Cliffs, N.J.: Prentice-Hall, Inc., 1972.

© Phiz Mezey

Chapter 14

IMPACT ON OPEN EDUCATION
FIFTY YEARS OF RESIDENT OUTDOOR EDUCATION: 1930-1980

by Esther P. Railton

Esther P. Railton, Ed.D.
Professor of Teacher Education
California State University, Hayward

Esther Railton coordinates an environmental option
in curriculum for master's degree candidates and
student teachers, and directs an environmental education laboratory. She has taught methods courses and
supervised student teachers. In addition, she teaches
advanced curriculum for all grades, pre-school
through post-secondary.

Dr. Railton co-authored *Teaching Science in an
Outdoor Environment* with Phyllis Gross, University
of California Press, 1972, and has a number of published articles. She is often called on to do consultant
work and speak at conferences. Dr. Railton has held
offices in the Association for Outdoor and Environmental Education, the American Nature Study Society
and the Conservation Education Association.

In 1976, the Howard Bell Award for leadership
from the Association for Outdoor and Environmental
Education was awarded to Dr. Railton. She has also
received merit certificates from the California Anti-
Litter League and the Institute for Environmental
Sciences. She is listed in *Who's Who in Education*,
the *World Directory of Environmental Education*,
Leaders in Outdoor Education, and other biblio-
graphies. She has received one national and two state
grants for her university.

Before moving to California in 1960, Dr. Railton
attended Western Michigan University, the University
of Michigan, Michigan State University, and the University of Illinois. She taught elementary and middle
school in Michigan. During the summers she taught
for universities in several states. One of her Michigan
assignments was Clear Lake Camp, where she
became acquainted with L. B. Sharp, Julian Smith,
and other leaders in outdoor education.

Years ago at Clear Lake Camp, the staff used to say that teachers who brought their children to outdoor schools were different when they went back to the classroom. At that time the writer wanted to quantify the empirical evidence, but in the 1950s nonparametric statistics and research related to teacher behavior were in their infancy. Now, however, classroom instruction has assumed a new character, taking on many of the attributes of the early outdoor schools.

It is interesting that the characteristics of open education almost exactly parallel the changes in classroom teachers after a week of outdoor education. In this chapter those characteristics are examined one by one to show how they are descriptive of both open education and outdoor education.

The history of both movements refutes the charge that either is an educational fad. The time lines support the assumption of parallelism. Outdoor education began in the 1930s and developed during the next two decades. Open education is often attributed to the British infant schools, starting in the 1950s based on some prototypes going back to the 1930s. During the 1960s American teachers began widespread study and adaptation of this system. Literature began to appear in rapid succession in the 1960s and evaluation began coming out in the 1970s.(13)

Philosophy

Both developments were influenced by the same philosophies—i.e., Dewey followed by Gessells, Jersild, Almy, Piaget, Erickson, and Bruner.(9) Both related to the child development psychology and humanistic education that followed World War II.(3)

The philosophy of open education and outdoor education have similar elements. One is self-selection. Both programs are available to anyone who is able to attend traditional schools, but participation is usually not mandatory. Teachers may be expected to take sixth grade children to camp in some districts, but generally they can select how much of the actual preparation and field instruction they want to direct, or they may even opt for substitute instructors or different grades. Student teachers and interns choose outdoor education as a part of their student teaching only if they want that option, and often they have to struggle for it. Likewise, high school counselors either volunteer or are selected for special leadership ability. While they go as a classroom unit, the campers need parent permission for overnight field trips and cannot legally be forced to go. This all means that there is a motivational freshness of free choice in the learning activities; therefore, the worst punishment is to be left out.

Despite the forebodings of academia, improved human relations remain the primary goal of both educational ventures. The school camps of the forties and fifties stressed this value, and recent concern about values education has brought us back to humanities in education. In both programs the teachers must be sensitive to the feelings of themselves and their pupils. Attitudes are considered as important as facts and skills.(2)

This humanistic trend extends to a concern about people. What is the effect of "quality of life" on a family whose "bread" may stop if a factory closes? Or conversely, what value is an affluent income with no remaining environmental products to purchase? It has been said that the endangered species may be human. Environmental interpreters need to be extremely sensitive to the reactions of people to the environment, remembering that people are a part of it, too, affected by it as well as affecting it. Children need to understand why we behave toward the environment in a certain way. They learn to link freedom to responsibility and consequences.(1)

Children's reactions to living together need to be discussed. How people live in the rural community, neighboring the outdoor school, and how people lived and felt about living in previous communities, learned through environmental living programs, are a part of both open and outdoor education.

Bremer lists the following among student goals for the Parkway Program of open education in Philadelphia:

To be effective in society
To develop skills of management in the community
To understand one's self and one's environment
To develop basic skills of language and mathematics, especially listening and speaking
To become self-propelling, responsible for one's own actions
To cooperate on teams
To learn what is useful
To become an inquisitive and open-minded individual
To develop initiative
To become process oriented
To become acquainted with the social organization of which one is a part.(1)

These compare with Sharp's emphasis on camper participation in planning, self-discovery, understanding of himself in a group and how people live together, solving useful problems of living, and emphasis on experience.(12) These goals lead to instruction and learning proceeding with an attitude of optimism, for the human is treated as an autonomous individual with control over his own destiny.

Curriculum

In keeping with the foregoing philosophy of humanism, one rightly expects the two types of education to have similar curricula. In fact, some open education schools, as in Boulder, Colorado, are called environmental schools. In each there is a strong emphasis on communication skills, especially those of speaking, listening, and writing. Reading is related to experience. In either program a schedule would be likely to include storytelling, dramatics, puppetry, poetry, and writing books and special dictionaries.

Social studies are focused on actual social situations—including the children's historical background and mechanisms of change. Construction projects might include building a kiosk or dome or making models of cities, buildings, machines, or playgrounds. Children make their own maps. They might be gardening, cooking the vegetables, or preserving fruit.

The children take excursions into the community and may base a whole semester's study on such an excursion or on a week at camp. For example, a Lafayette, California class camped in the coastal redwoods near an old stagecoach station where the railroad bed from early logging was still visible. A creative teacher, Elizabeth Timmers, picked up on the idea that in the environs of metropolitan Oakland, where the district is located, the children could study redwood logging as part of their own community history. This led the class to an old newspaper account describing the largest redwood stump recorded anywhere within the school district. The children found and mapped the location of that stump. The related logging history turned out to be even more exciting than camp and served as a curriculum core for months. This is an example of outdoor and open education inseparably combined.

Science and social studies often furnish the topics for research, discussion, and activity. A store or trading post can be the beginning of comparison shopping, classifying products, writing and reading labels, subtracting from a balance, and accounting. It can also be a place to practice friendliness, courtesy, and accurate English.

Mathematics and science are taught in functional situations as the need arises. Concepts of numbers are at least as important as computation. Children use their arms or body length to measure a pole. Shadows are paced off to estimate the height of a tree. Recently the author watched third graders with rulers measure a

kindergarten annex for a model of the school they were building. Science may center around a wind or water mill or a solar collector. One boy, who had gone to sixth grade camp and afterwards was involved in an energy project, asked, "If you took the pickup a few miles to cut a load of firewood, would you use more BTU's than you brought home?" Nature trails furnish study of ecological interrelationships, the significance of structure in function, in addition to taxonomy of familiar phenomena. As in gardening, geology, soil science, meteorology, entomology, and botany, cycles form a succession of units. Constellations are seen in the outdoor school skies, or the children in an open school bring sleeping bags and observe them from the school lawn.

Music and art are important elements of a program that emphasizes humanities. Children make their own instruments to play their own compositions. They weave, sew, or tie macrame.

Play is an accepted part of both types of curriculum. The children play games suitable to the outdoor environment, such as fox and geese, lacrosse, or capture the flag. During a quiet period they bring out checkers, scrabble, dominoes, and homemade games. The new games where everybody wins fit into the philosophy of noncompetitiveness.

Methods of Learning

In the preceding examples, the curriculum is action-based. Learning is organized around firsthand experiences. The child discovers, manipulates, plans, questions, and practices things important to him, progressing from the known to the new.(9) The basic *strategy* for such a curriculum is problem solving. Children are led to observe changes and to be a part of happenings. They try out things to discover how they work.

An important characteristic of open education, which also characterizes the lively outdoor schools that sustain community support, is that children plan their work. They are involved in decision making. The learners select their own activities with the teacher's guidance to assure that they are developmentally appropriate. There is a need to balance what children do want with what children should want. Accordingly, in order to keep its educational commitment, the program must not neglect the three Rs.

The children act out the environment; they determine the effect their actions have on it. They abstract information and operate on this information. Dialogue is important to clarify the significance of the activities.(3) Learning in a community context helps learners understand how learning is relevant to their world. However, as in the Lafayette illustration, learners and teachers do not automatically relate their own community, the outdoor school community, and the world community.

The processes of outdoor learning and open instruction are based on inquiry, discovery, and active connections that improve memory.(10) Some of these active processes are detecting patterns, building models, interacting, creating, measuring, inferring, predicting, experimenting, and research. These are associated with such psychomotor processes as walking, using tools, drawing, and typing. Equally important are the affective responses of selecting, rejecting, enjoying, and being neat.(9)

Organization of Instruction

The organization of instruction for outdoor education varies from program to program, but it has evolved along the same lines as open education. Small ad hoc groups form the instructional unit, polarized around interests. These groups may change according to the activity.

As already mentioned, planning is done by the group, and a flexible planning schedule is filled in to assure time to meet the goals of the learners. However, the outdoor or building coordinator must help the learners fit the parts together into a logical order. Relationships need to be established between what children already know and new material. Therefore, a teacher appointed to lead the students through a series of experiences is preferable to having each outdoor activity taught by a different "subject specialist."

Staff

To conduct the programs described, the teacher's role is quite different from that of a lecturer or grader of papers. The teacher must be an adventurer, for he or she is breaking tradition to set up a situation with an unknown outcome. In doing so, the teacher becomes an advisor, an innovator, a resource rather than a giver of knowledge. Another role of the teacher is that of a co-ordinator, working with a team of other teachers. In open and outdoor schools, volunteer leadership is almost essential for an adequate staff. These persons may be people from the community, such as the custodian who could help cut a tree. They may be student teachers or interns or high school counselors and aides.

Parents are welcome in open education, and outdoor teachers would do well to include them if they wish to maintain their support in times of budget cuts. In one incipient program, parents furnished the dining room staff and did some teaching related to their expertise or hobbies. This was after they had organized the fund raising and convinced the administration that the program should be approved.

The teacher needs to be a persuader, to convince colleagues they should participate or to assure them that they need not, as the case may be. The teacher needs to explain to the principal why recess does not have to be at a given bell time or to show the school board that videotaping a film is indeed writing composition. One teacher sells industry the idea that his mentally retarded high school students should work as custodians and that the same boys, on a field trip, can sleep within a factory's security fence.

Thus the teacher must work with a variety of people. The instructional emphasis is on how, not what, children learn. The outdoor or open teacher is an experimenter.

The administrator is described well by Kathleen Devaney, a consultant at the Far West Laboratory.

> The position of the advisor (outdoor education teacher) seems similar to that of the curriculum coordinator or specialist . . . but. . . the advisor's objective is to "look for growing points" from which to develop the teacher's professional skill, rather than to evaluate the teacher; and the advisor's activities are the actual teaching of teachers and children rather than administering official policies and installing officially adopted programs.(3)

This description was published in 1974, but the potential of the outdoor education teacher as a teacher-trainer has not been explored.

Physical Equipment and Instructional Material

This kind of program, whether in a school or a camp, requires different physical equipment from the standard classroom. Outdoor education is based on using the environment provided by nature as instructional material with a minimum of added supplies. These supplies for either program are often scrap or inexpensive and of a versatile nature, such as boxes, string, glue, and a few basic tools such as saws, hammers, and rulers. Children may bring materials. For example, clay is found in the field or stream bank; sawdust for puppet sculpture is collected on a visit to a lumber mill. Despite the return to the basics pressure, this cost feature is significant to the survival of outdoor and open education in the current fiscal crisis.

In outdoor and open education, the classroom has no partitions; it extends as far as the class can walk. It may resemble a wood shop, a sandpile or a store. Activity centers are common features. They will include live plants and animals, with magnifying glasses and microscopes within easy reach. Audiovisual equipment is needed for production as well as for showing filmstrips and videotapes.

The essential nature of the materials for instruction is that they are common, inexpensive, familiar, and of many potential uses. They cause puzzlement or give ideas. For example, at Clear Lake, Michigan, children climb a stile built by fellow campers about thirty years ago, appreciating the enduring contribution to the community that people like themselves can make. A classic inquiry center is a tree stump about which at least twenty questions can be asked. (If outdoor teachers used the term "inquiry center" instead of "teaching station," the process of learning would be improved.)

Evaluation

Evaluations of pupils and student teachers do not compare individuals with their peers. There are no grades or report cards. Success in reaching goals is measured by the children themselves, and as soon as they begin to ask why they did or did not reach them, they are evaluating processes. If skillfully led, the pupils even devise the remedial techniques that are necessary. In open education, teachers evaluate students; students evaluate the program, themselves, and the teacher; and parents evaluate the program. A recent evaluating tool

© Phiz Mezey

for outdoor education in California is based on self-appraisal. Sample evaluation forms are provided for the outdoor administrator, the outdoor teacher, the classroom teacher, the pupils, and the parents.(7)

Problems

Problems of evaluation have been the stumbling blocks to acceptance of outdoor and open education. Until recently neither outdoor nor open schools have had clear goals and objectives. One reason is that the philosophy of these schools requires a different set of objectives for each group. When clear goals were present, they were not accompanied by specific criteria for judging achievement.(12) Most schools have no data from control groups. An additional problem, illustrated by the field research of Margaret Kelley, is that the experimental teachers are not always using the discovery processes just because they teach outdoors or lead an activity, even though they report they do. Conversely, the control teachers may be using open techniques.(8)

Perusal of numerous evaluations of open and outdoor programs find parallel lists of observation data, interview data, and questionnaire surveys of children, parents, counselors, teachers, and administrators. All of these provide subjective data.

Neither type of education has an "accepted" curriculum on paper, therefore they share a nebulous existence. This has a plus factor, for they will exist in whole or part only so long as they are functional. However, good may be thrown out in curricular housecleaning because it does not fit a labeled shelf.

Neither program has an agreed upon definition. Discussions have bogged down, and treatises not worth their paper have been written about the proper terminology and definitive characteristics of each. In case the reader demands some definitions, Good's *Dictionary of Education* may suffice for outdoor education, but there is no entry in the third edition for open education, only "classrooms, open."

Outdoor Education: An approach to teaching and a process through which learning experiences in all areas of the educational curriculum are provided and in which natural, community, and human resources beyond the traditional classroom are utilized as a motivation for learning and a means of broad curriculum enrichment and vitalization; direct firsthand learning opportunities involve the teacher and student in ecological explorations of the environment to develop and/or improve the knowledge, understanding, attitude, behavior, appreciation, values, skills, and stewardship responsibility of the learner; education in, for, and about the physical and biotic environment is emphasized in order to achieve a wide variety of educational goals.(5)

About open education, David Nyberg, a philosopher of education, has written:

> *Open education* is that form of educational practice which is characteristically regulated by the following rules:
>
> 1. Students are to pursue educational activities of their own choosing;
> 2. Teachers are to create an environment rich in educational possibilities;
> 3. Teachers are to give a student individualized instruction based on what he/she is interested in, but they are also to guide the student along educationally worthwhile lines;
> 4. Teachers are to respect students. The following count as exhibiting respect for the student:
>   *a.* the student is granted considerable freedom; he/she is, for the most part, autonomous,
>   *b.* the student's interests and ideas are considered to be important and he/she receives individual instruction and guidance based on his/her interests,
>   *c.* there is considerable interaction between teacher and students; they are considered equal in some sense,
>   *d.* students are rarely commanded; uses of authority are minimized,
>   *e.* students' feelings are to be taken seriously.(11)

With regard to teachers' roles on an instructional team, there are problems of agreement as to objectives, materials, who determines rules and procedures, and what is acceptable conduct. Probably more outdoor school staff problems have centered on the operation of the dining hall than on all instructional strategies put together.

There are great demands on the teacher in either program; that is probably why patience snaps over a dirty sponge on a table. The teacher has to be voluntarily in either kind of program. Administrative support is essential but must not be mandated. Principals and directors may be narrow, unable to deal with staff ideas on curricular change. Furthermore, administrators and parents may not always understand, therefore, as Myers points out, autonomy may lead to opposition.(9) On the other hand, the teachers' interests, so important in the development of activity-centered instruction, may be biased or warped. The free atmosphere of either school may too readily furnish an arena for teachers to impose their personal antisocial feelings on a captive audience. Either program must be consistant with the ideals of an orderly democratic society.

Summary

In summary, the correlations between open education and outdoor education are too parallel to support the notion of chance. They are:

1. A philosophy of human values in an open society
2. Curriculum organized in an interdisciplinary manner around problems with skills taught as needed
3. Instructional strategies of inquiry and discovery with open-ended questions
4. Organization for small group instruction and team leadership, with flexible schedules
5. The role of the teacher as a member of the group
6. Physical characteristics of open space and multi-use materials
7. Difficulty in objective evaluation without peer comparisons
8. Problems of definition, administration, and finance

Both occurred within the past fifty years with open education following outdoor education by about ten years. Some day a study should be made to determine if a significant proportion of teachers and administrators who set up open classrooms had outdoor education experience.

Selected References

1. Bremer, John and von Moschzisker, Michael. *The School Without Walls, Philadelphia's Parkway Program.* New York: Holt, Rinehart and Winston, Inc., 1969.
2. Bussis, Anne M., and Chittenden, Edward A. *Analysis of an Approach to Open Education.* Princeton: Educational Testing Service, 1970.
3. Devaney, Kathleen. *Developing Open Education in America.* Washington, D.C.: National Association for the Education of Young Children, 1974.
4. Duke, Daniel Londen and Muzio, Irene. "How Effective Are Alternative Schools? A Review of Recent Evaluations and Reports." *Teachers College Record,* February 1978.
5. Good, Carter V. (ed.) *Dictionary of Education,* Third Edition. New York: McGraw-Hill, 1973, p. 404.

6. Gross, Phyllis and Railton, Esther P. *Teaching Science in an Outdoor Environment.* Berkeley: University of California Press, 1972.
7. "Guide for Self-Appraisal and Certification of Resident Outdoor Environmental Education Programs." Downey, California: the Office of the Los Angeles County Superintendent of Schools, n.d.
8. Kelley, Margaret. *A Guide to Quantifying Experimental Learning in Outdoor Education.* Unpublished master's thesis, San Jose State University, 1979.
9. Myers, Donald A., and Myers, Lilian. *Open Education Reexamined.* Massachusetts: Lexington Books, 1973.
10. Norman, Donald. *Memory and Attention: An Introduction to Human Information Processing.* New York: Wiley and Sons, 1969.
11. Nyberg, David. *The Philosophy of Open Education.* London and Boston: Routledge & Kegan Paul, Ltd., 1975, p. 17.
12. Sharp, L. B. "Basic Considerations in Outdoor Camping Education." *The Bulletin of the National Association of Secondary School Principals.* May, 1974. pp. 43-47.
13. Spodek, Bernard and Walberg, Herbert J. (eds). *Studies in Open Education.* New York: Agathon Press, 1975.

© Phiz Mezey

Chapter 15

IMPACT ON EDUCATIONAL RESEARCH
FIFTY YEARS OF RESIDENT OUTDOOR EDUCATION: 1930-1980

by Betty van der Smissen

Dr. Betty van der Smissen, Re.D.

Director, School of Health, Physical
    Education and Recreation
Bowling Green State University, Ohio

Betty van der Smissen has been actively involved in outdoor education for twenty-five years. She participated as a graduate student in outdoor education programs and studied at Indiana University in the early years of the development of Bradford Woods, Indiana University.

While at the University of Iowa for eight years, Dr. van der Smissen taught courses on outdoor education and advised graduate studies. She became involved in research and directed the first workshop on Research Related to Camping sponsored by the American Camping Association in 1963 and compiled the first bibliography on camping research that was published by ACA in 1962, supplement 1965. She served on the ACA Board of Directors as national research chairperson. At the University of Iowa, she was the first director of Macbride Field Campus, after working on the land negotiations and master plan for the area. She also utilized the Outdoor Project (outing sports) of the Council of Outdoor Education and Camping, AAHPER. With Ozwald Goering she co-authored the book, *A Leader's Guide to Nature-Oriented Activities,* which was published in 1965. She also produced a filmstrip series (8) with an instructor's manual on campcraft.

She went to The Pennsylvania State University in 1965 and continued to be involved in outdoor education programs for the fourteen years she remained there. The University had an area, Stone Valley Recreation Area; and, it was together with Dr. Fred Coombs, chairman of Recreation and Parks, that the Area was further developed. She provided leadership for the Area's outdoor education program and following federal and state funding, a year-round outdoor education program servicing schools in the Commonwealth was conducted until 1978, when the program was cut-back.

Dr. van der Smissen's work in teaching and research expanded significantly and she led in the development of academic programs in the outdoor field at the bachelor's, master's, and doctoral levels. Her work focused on the graduate program, both in teaching seminars and directing research. Her interest in research continued and she updated the Bibliography of Research in 1970 and 1979. She also initiated and co-directed two research symposiums on Camping and Environmental Education in 1975 and 1979, both of which resulted in major proceedings' volumes.

Dr. van der Smissen continued to be active in professional organizations. She was chairman of the American Camping Association task force on outdoor education and in such capacity served on the national board. The ACA honored her in 1976 with the Hedley S. Dimock Award for contributions to camping through education.

As well as maintaining research and professional organization involvements, as a lawyer she is very active in both speaking and writing about the legal liability of outdoor programs. In addition to several articles published, she has written a document on *Legal Liability—Adventure Activities,* published by ERIC (1980), and a book *Legal Liabilities of Cities and Schools.*

At Bowling Green State University (Ohio), Dr. van der Smissen is involved in the Environmental Studies program. She currently (1980-82) serves as national president of the American Camping Association.

The research related to resident outdoor education over fifty years is reflective of the movement and may be divided into four eras characterized as:

Camping as Education   — prior to the 1950s
School Camping   — the 1950s
Outdoor Education   — the later 1950s and 1960s
Environmental Education — the 1970s

The title of this chapter indicates discussion of the *impact* of resident outdoor education on educational research; however, an analysis of the research relating to resident outdoor education shows little actual impact on educational research. Rather, what will be discussed is the nature of the research in each of the four eras. This will not be a review of the content of the research, that is, individual studies will not be presented.

The percentage of studies referenced for the categories of research within the eras are based upon an analysis of the most recent compilation of research, van der Smissen (1979), which endeavored to incorporate all known source information into one master bibliography. It is the only bibliography known which has included studies prior to 1950. For the purpose of citing percentages, an effort was made to identify those studies which appeared to be concerned with resident outdoor education settings. While it is difficult to do so, approximately 300, or 20 percent, of the citations were selected based on title and author's familiarity with the research.

I. Camping as Education, Prior to 1950

The first era, before the 1950s, was characterized by organized camp leaders who believed in the educational values of resident camping endeavoring to impact upon education by working with influential education leaders in prestigious institutions. The work of these people established the foundation for resident outdoor education.

In 1922 Dr. Charles Eliot, president emeritus of Harvard University, then 88 years old, in talking of the values of camping stated, "The organized summer camp is the greatest contribution America has made to education."

At this same meeting of the National Association of Directors of Girls Private Camps, the topic "Future of Camping in Relation to the Schools" was discussed by Eleanor Derrying. In closing she said, "Let us supplement the school and the city life, so that the wise Commissioner of Education will awaken to the fact that the camp is fully as important as the School—."(8)

Organized camping leaders continued their interest in and concern for camping as an educational institution. In 1927 at an annual convention, the theme "Home, School and Camp" was used and the sessions emphasized the educational changes of the past ten years and the new Columbia theory of education with spontaneous activity and creative self-expression.

Again in 1929, the convention focused on education. At this meeting a committee (organized in 1928) of the New York Section of the American Camping Association, with Ralph C. Hill, as chairman, presented a pamphlet which it had prepared entitled "The Place of the Organized Summer Camp in Education." Some people felt that this was one of the most important documents from the organized camping movement.(8) "It recognized the continuous nature of education and described the kind of camp climate that best contributes to the growth of children and young people. In 1945, after the original pamphlet had been out of print for many years, a second New York Section committee, chaired by Frederick L. Guggenheimer who had done his master's thesis on this topic, published a new edition without any radical changes stating, 'The theories and principles developed then seem, with very slight modification, to be as sound now as they were thought to be then.' "(4)

Later in 1959 the pamphlet was again reviewed, and while the basic philosophy and general principles were retained, it was updated to reflect the development of educational theory over the last quarter century.

The research of this era reflected the interest of organized camping leaders in camping as an educational institution and the studies focused on the assessment of camping's educational values. The first dissertation on record was completed in 1925 by Alcott F. Elwell, who was then a graduate student at Harvard University and was one of four speakers at the aforementioned 1922 meeting. His study was entitled "The Summer Camp: A New Factor in Education." A second dissertation was completed at the University of Southern California in 1928 by James S. Arnold, who wrote on "The Educational Possibilities of the Summer Camp Program."

One of the most prominent leaders in outdoor education has been L. B. Sharp. In 1930 he was with the Department of Education at the University of Chicago and was named chairman of a committee on National Camp Federation. At this time, he wrote his doctoral dissertation at Columbia University entitled "Education and the Summer Camp—An Experiment." It was published that year under the same title as "Contributions to Education," No. 390, by Teachers College, Columbia University.

Also in 1930 another prominent outdoor leader, Bernard S. Mason, completed his doctoral dissertation entitled "Camping and Education" at The Ohio State

University. The next year, 1931, three additional academic studies were completed:

Adams, Luch Harding, "How Summer Camps for Girls Serve the Purposes and Aims of Education." Master's thesis, Texas Christian University.

Houck, Ivan D. "The American Camp Movement: Its Educational and Social Significance." Master's thesis, Temple University.

Guggenheimer, Frederick L. "The Camp and the New Education." Master's thesis, Teachers College, Columbia University.

. . . and there were three more studies in 1934:

Day, Robert Fuller. "The Organized Summer Camp for Boys as an Educational Agency." Master's thesis, Brown University.

Heinlen, Lois B. "A Study of the Educational Values of Organized Summer Camps for Adolescents." Master's thesis, The Ohio State University.

McAuliffe, Florence J. "The Summer Camp—A Contribution to Education." Master's thesis, Boston College.

One other master's thesis (no doctoral dissertation) is recorded prior to 1940: Bushman, William W. "The Educational Values of Summer Camps for Boys." Southern Methodist University.

In the 1930s and 1940s resident outdoor education programs, as described in other chapters, were being developed throughout the country. Mrs. Johanna M. Lindlof, chairman of the Committee on Instructional Affairs of the Board of Education of the City of New York, instigated a resident camping program and the evaluation of four years of programs was set forth in the pamphlet entitled "Adventures in Camping."(13) This program was developed in conjunction with L. B. Sharp, who had established Life Camps. Subsequently, in 1947 the New York Board of Education passed a resolution entitled "Experiment in Continued Education Through Camping." The report of the study was published by the Board of Education of the City of New York.(10) This study has become a classic, and Julian Smith stated that there was really no need for further research because this study proved so conclusively the value of the resident outdoor education program to education. While many would not go that far, there is little question that the study represented one of the first experimental studies and provided a sound foundation in support of camping as an educational experience for school children.

At about this same time, the W. K. Kellogg Founda-

tion supported an experimental project through the Experimental Division of Health, Physical Education, Recreation, School Camping, and Outdoor Education of the Department of Public Instruction. This project was under the leadership of Hugh B. Masters of Kellogg Foundation and Julian Smith of the Department of Public Instruction.(9) In 1946, the city and county of San Diego began its camping program. The results of its first program, Camp Cuyamaca, and the second, Palomar Mountain Camp, are reported in a 1951 book.(5) George Peabody College for Teachers also conducted experimental programs and concluded: "The counselors, children and parents were convinced that these phases of education (tangible—knowledge of nature, how to prepare food, safety, camp crafts, planning programs; intangible—group cooperation, knowing each other better, knowing other people,

© Phiz Mezey

independence, good time, better social adjustment) could not have been accomplished so well in the classroom as they were in camp.''(6)

In this first era the focus was on camping as education, and the research generally was supported by the official education body (e.g., department or board of education) in an effort to assess the resident camping experience as education. The interest of the official educational bodies was manifest in the professional periodicals, which devoted special issues during this time to camping education.(1, 2, 3)

While few reported studies by operational programs seem to have been identified, other than the four aforementioned, there were six additional academic studies reported from 1945 to 1948 and seven in the 1950s which focused on camping as education.(21) As described later, the research seemed to shift from the more broad concern of camping as education prior to 1950s to specific outcomes from outdoor education experiences in the later 1950s to 1980.

II. School Camping, Decade of the 50s

In the years before 1950, the leadership focused on determining the values of the organized resident camp in terms of educational principles. Once these seem to have been established with the educational leadership, attention was turned to the operation of school camp programs. This era is really a brief transition period from the more basic educational outcomes and the use of the name ''school camping'' to the broad program operations of ''outdoor education'' in a resident setting which began in the latter part of the 1950s and extended until about 1970. Seven studies in the 1950s continued to investigate camping as education, but more than 30 theses and dissertations focused on the operational aspects of the school camp. The shift in terminology was so complete by 1960 that only two studies in the 60s and two in the 70s were identified which used the term ''school camping.''(21)

III. Outdoor Education, the Latter 1950s and the 1960s

The research of this era is characterized by two quite different concerns: (a) operations, and (b) evaluation of ''innovative'' outdoor education programs. About the first, George Donaldson said, ''Research in outdoor education almost appears to have been conducted on the basis of what is easiest to study rather than in answer to 'what needs to be known.' Such a criterion would explain the undue research emphasis upon the resi-

dent . . . aspect of outdoor education. It might also explain the early preponderance of administrative studies.''(7) The second concern was occasioned by the requirement of the federal government for an evaluation component in Title III Projects.

There were more than 130 master's theses and doctoral dissertations focusing on outdoor education in this era. Almost all of these fall within the concern of operations, and may be generally classified into four types: administration, general surveys, proposed programs, and curriculum articulation. Not quite one-half of the studies are within the administration field, and include manuals, organizational structure, personnel, et al. The other studies are fairly equally divided among the other three types.

In an effort to know what was going on both nationwide and in specific states, at least fifteen of the studies, mostly in the latter 50s, were surveys. Much of the research was very specific to one program in all of the other three types. Studies of proposed programs outlined the development and structure of a program for a given school. Many of the administration studies also were specific to operational concerns of a given school. Because these studies were so operationally-specific, they had little impact on educational research in general.

While one might anticipate that the curriculum articulation studies might make a contribution to educational research or at least utilize educational research methodology, a review of many of the studies indicates this is not so. Most of the studies merely identified activities suitable for curriculum areas; furthermore, in this era most of the studies did not consider student outcomes. In these studies, as well as the aforementioned three types, there appears to be little depth or conceptual consideration, perhaps because of the extreme emphasis upon operational programs.

While these curriculum studies apparently were done in part to help ''sell'' an outdoor education program to school boards through justifying the program in terms of the curriculum areas, such aims were not totally successful. It should be noted that in the first era prior to the 1950s the research approached the resident camp as education, in terms of educational principles. In this era, however, individual activities appropriate to various subject areas were identified. Also, it appears that the close working relationship between educators (educational administrators) and the camp administrators of the first era was lost in the 1950s.

In the mid-60s the nature of the research shifted when the funding base and approach changed in order to take advantage of the ESEA legislation for innovative education programs. Approximately 100 of the 130 theses and dissertations were done before the mid-60s (1966). At first a strong evaluation component was not required in proposals under Title III of ESEA; later evaluation was more strongly emphasized. However, it is generally considered that at no time was research really integral to these "innovative projects" and that the evaluation components were ineffective for the most part. Commonly a project was evaluated by "writing up" what happened and providing some statistics—not evaluating what had actually occurred, either in terms of process or student outcomes.

ERIC/CRESS (Clearinghouse on Rural Education and Small Schools, New Mexico State University) endeavored to compile information on outdoor education programs, and the first bibliography appeared in March 1970 with annual supplements thereafter.(11) While this Center has done a commendable job in compiling and disseminating outdoor education information, little of it is either research or research-related.

The federal government through the New Jersey State Council for Environmental Education funded a National Conference on Environmental Education that was held in May 1968. A conference working paper "Evaluation for Environmental Education" was prepared which presumably dealt with a systems analysis approach for self-evaluation.(14) This document attempted to outline some standards in the areas of planning and design, content, operation, and productivity. It was almost totally operations-oriented, and had little information concerning the measurement of student outcomes.

While this era of Outdoor Education may be considered the "golden era" for the development of residential programs, because of the tremendous obsession with programming, little appears to have been contributed to education research.

IV. Environmental Education, the 1970s

The transition of terminology is quite complete to "environmental education" in the research, with only a couple of studies in the 70s referring to "school camping" and approximately fifteen studies to "outdoor education." While there is a considerable quantity of literature regarding environmental education in the 1970s, little of it is concerned with research of residential programs.(19) Although it is difficult to identify resident-oriented environmental education studies, about a dozen seem to be on administration and program in general. Most of the research, however, is characterized by focusing on specific topics. This approach is in direct contrast to the previous eras. The largest number (about thirty) of the theses and dissertations on environmental

education endeavor to assess outcomes. Other studies are concerned with methodology evaluation, use of outdoor programs for special populations, and development of environmental centers. Roth classifies environmental studies as a whole into these categories: environmental education concepts and programs, curriculum and program development, simulations—gaming—and—modeling, evaluation instruments, investigation of teachers' attitudes toward environmental education concepts, teacher education, camp programs, administration guidelines-practices, facilities and sites, and environmental communications.(17) This listing gives some idea of the wide scope of environmental education research today (1980).

The educational field has given emphasis to behavioral competencies and individuality. This is reflected in the larger number of studies dealing with specific types of outcomes through an environmental education program. However, this is not totally a phenomenon of the 70s. In the 1950s there were at least a dozen studies dealing with different outcomes. The oldest study cited in the van der Smissen 1979 bibliography is a dissertation done by Arthur C. Brown in 1918 entitled "A Study of Character Building" at the University of Southern California. The largest categories of outcomes are values and value clarification, environmental attitudes, and social behavior, especially self-concept. In 1975, Iida identified 327 studies related to resident settings (both camping and education), 35 percent in the 60s and 43 percent in the 70s.(12) About one-half were concerned with outcomes of the experience.

The social-educational philosophy of the 70s also encompasses the rights of special populations. Very few studies were done in Era III concerning special populations; however, in Eras I and II there was considerable interest, especially in interracial camping. While most of the studies concerning special populations do not refer to environmental education, one of the most rapidly growing fields of camping is that of therapeutic camping. The Iida study identified about 100 studies in residential settings concerned with special populations. There is also considerable research to determine the effects of programs and the appropriate strategies to use.

Whereas in Era III there were many studies concerned with curriculum, it was in terms of activities for subject areas. In Era IV the curriculum-related studies focus on methodology.

In conducting the research related to behavioral outcomes, special populations, and methodology, there appears to be a return to working with not only educational researchers (as in Era I) but also with researchers in psychology, social psychology, sociology, child development, etc. In fact, much of the research is being done in those fields, in contrast to the research in Era III that was done primarily by practitioners or would-be practitioners in outdoor education programs, most of whom had little background in the basic disciplines. The research in Era III was entirely practical-oriented, rather than theory-testing or conceptual-oriented.

What is the Impact on Educational Research?

After fifty years perhaps residential outdoor education researchers are finally becoming research partners with educational researchers and researchers in the basic disciplines. The research seems to be focusing on more specific objectives, thus permitting more sophisticated research designs. This appears to be fostered by the genuine concern for individual growth and development through the educational system and supplemental systems, such as alternative education programs of which the residential outdoor setting is, or can be, a major contributor. The research problem also appears to be directed toward the testing of theory, rather than just an assessment of a desirable operational practice—the questions being asked are WHY and HOW.

If the "golden era" of residential outdoor education programs is to return, there must be not only more sophisticated "proof" of being able to meet certain objectives (outcomes for participants), but also more strategies based on conceptual rationale rather than operating primarily on "experience-wisdom." There also must be more research building upon previous research, rather than each study being isolated, as so much of the research to date has been (one need only to read a study's review of literature). A body of research knowledge must be built and then translated into program reality.

© Phiz Mezey

Selected References

1. "Camping and Outdoor Education" (edited by L. B. Sharp and E. DeAlton Partridge). *The Bulletin* of the National Association of Secondary-School Principals, vol. 31, no. 147, May 1947.
2. "Camping and Outdoor Education" (edited by Jay B. Nash, Milton A. Gabrielsen, Arthur W. Selverstone). *The Journal of Educational Sociology*, vol. 23, no. 9, May 1950.
3. "Camping Education for the Elementary School Child." *The National Elementary Principal*, vol. XXVIII, no. 4, February 1949.
4. *Camping is Education.* Martinsville, Indiana: American Camping Association, 1960, p. 5.
5. Clarke, James M. "California's Pilot Project in Outdoor Education." *Public School Camping.* Stanford, California: Stanford University Press, 1951.
6. DeWitt, R. T. "Camping Education—A Philosophy." *The National Elementary Principal*, vol. XXVIII, no. 4, February 1949, pp. 3-5.
7. Donaldson, George W. "A Position Paper: Research Utilization in Outdoor Education." Las Cruces, N.M.: New Mexico State University, ERIC/CRESS. September 1970.
8. Eells, Eleanor. Notes on history of organized camping.
9. Elliott, Eugene B., and Smith, Julian W., "The Michigan Program in Action." *The Bulletin.* National Association of Secondary-School Principals, May 1947, pp. 60-74.
10. *Extending Education Through Camping.* Report of the School Camp Experiment. New York, N.Y.: Life Camps, 1948.
11. Fulton, Eulyne, and Loomis, Charlotte Ann, compilers. "Outdoor Education, A Selected Bibliography," March 1970. Also annual supplements. Las Cruces, N.M.: New Mexico State University, ERIC/CRESS.
12. Iida, Minoru. "Bibliography of Research Related to Camping and Environmental Education in the Resident Setting as the Outdoor Experience Affects the Participant." In van der Smissen, Betty, compiler, *Research: Camping and Environmental Education.* Penn State HPER Series No. 11, 1975, pp. 468-508.
13. Johanna M. Lindlof Camp Committee for Public School Children. *Adventure in Camping.* New York City: the Committee. 1943.
14. New Jersey State Council for Environmental Education. Conference Working Paper: "Evaluation for Environmental Education (A Systems Analysis Approach for Self-Evaluation). Newark, N.J.: the Council. 1968.
15. Research in Outdoor Education, "Summaries of Doctoral Studies." Washington, D.C.: AAHPER. 1973.
16. Research Related to Camping. "Proceedings of Workshop," March 1963. Martinsville, Indiana: American Camping Association. 1964.
17. Roth, Robert E. "A Review of Research Related to Environmental Education, 1973-1976." Columbus, Ohio: The Ohio State University, ERIC Information Analysis Center for Science, Mathematics, and Environmental Education. 1976.
18. Roth, Robert E., and Helgeson, Stanley L., "A Review of Research Related to Environmental Education." Columbus, Ohio: The Ohio State University, ERIC Information Analysis Center for Science, Mathematics, and Environmental Education. September 1972.
19. Roth, Robert E., et al. *Environmental Education*, a Bibliography of Abstracts from Resources in Education (RIE) 1973-1975. Columbus, Ohio: Science, Mathematics, and Environmental Education. 1976.
20. Swan, Malcolm; Stark, William; Hammerman, Donald; and Lewis, Charles, compilers. "Research in Outdoor Education: Summaries of Doctoral Studies." Washington, D.C.: Council on Outdoor Education of the AAHPER. January 1978.
21. van der Smissen, Betty, compiler. "Bibliography of Research in Camping, Environmental Education, and Interpretive Services." Martinsville, Indiana: American Camping Association, 1979.
22. van der Smissen, Betty, compiler. "Bibliography Related to Camping and Outdoor Education." Martinsville, Indiana: American Camping Association, 1962 with 1965 supplement.
23. van der Smissen, Betty and Joyce, Donald V., editors. "Bibliography of Theses and Dissertations in Recreation, Parks, Camping and Outdoor Education," Washington, D.C.: National Recreation and Park Association, 1970.
24. Voelker, Alan M.; Heal, Fred A.; and Horvat, Robert E., "Environmental Education—Related Research, 1969-72 An Annotated Bibliography." Madison, Wisc.: University of Wisconsin-Madison, Center for Environmental Communications and Education Studies, n.d.
25. Vogl, Robert L., and Vogl, Sonia, "Outdoor Education and Its Contributions to Environmental Quality—A Research Analysis." ERIC/CRESS May 1974. Austin, Texas: National Educational Laboratory Publishers, Inc.

© Phiz Mezey

Chapter 16

IMPACT ON THE NATION'S SCHOOL
FIFTY YEARS OF RESIDENT OUTDOOR EDUCATION: 1930-1980

by William M. Hammerman

© Phiz Mezey

© Laura Huff

© Phiz Mezey

The impact of any educational movement is quite often documented by quantitative information regarding the number of people who have participated. Literature was searched in an effort to record references about the number of children and the number of school districts involved with resident outdoor education programs in various states. In 1935, during the Period of Inception (1930-1939), the U.S. Office of Education reported that six cities were sponsoring summer camp projects under the jurisdiction of their boards of education.(4) Many references were made about the growing acceptance of the value of camping experiences to education, but no statistical data was recorded.

In the twelve-year span labelled the Period of Experimentation (1940-1951), nine states were identified as states providing leadership in the early development of school camp programs: California, Florida, Indiana, Michigan, New Jersey, Ohio, Oregon, Pennsylvania, and Washington. By mid-century, more than forty school systems had experimented with school camping, and approximately twenty-three school camps were in operation.(1)

The impact of school camping was significant during the Period of Standardization (1952-1960), which was characterized by very rapid expansion of programs across the nation. In 1952, camping education had grown in the State of Michigan to the point where seventy school systems had incorporated at least one week of camping into the regular curriculum. California reported that 13,356 children from 269 schools in forty-six different school districts attended a resident outdoor education center during the 1953-54 school year. By the end of this period, 1959-60, these figures for California increased to 38,966 children from 586 schools in 190 school districts.(2)

According to a 1958 survey conducted in New Jersey, twenty-six public school districts offered outdoor education experiences for pupils. Also in 1958, Janet St. Clair reported in "The Growth, Development and Present Status of School Camping in the United States," that there were 109 resident camping programs (from four to seven days) in twenty-four states, and 33 two-to-four-day camping programs in ten states.(5) In her thesis, St. Clair concluded that of the ninety-two schools sponsoring programs meeting her criteria of having a four-to-seven-day program, including pupils from grades three through eight, and operating during normal school time, that:(6)

a. most (75 or 82%) of the school camps were established between 1950 and 1958; and
b. seventeen (18%) were started between 1937 and 1950.

Although these ninety-two programs were located in twenty-three different states, the majority were concentrated in the following five states: California (21), Michigan (14), Wisconsin (9), New York (8), and Ohio (8). By 1960, according to Julian Smith, over 600 school districts in the United States were participating, on an annual basis, in resident outdoor education programs.(1)

Until now, no national survey had ever been conducted regarding the status of school camping in America. The Period of New Directions (1970-1979) started with the results of a pilot survey, conducted by the NEA Research Division, being reported by Project Man's Environment. This study was conducted in public schools (K-12) in 1969-70 and covered 90 percent of all public school pupils in the nation.(3) It only included school systems, however, with enrollments of 1,000 pupils or more, and had the equivalent of at least one half-time staff member assigned to a program in the area of environmental education. From the 5,173 responding districts (7,143 inquiries were mailed), 781 school systems met the criteria for the study. The survey instrument was returned by 702 districts. The summary of the findings revealed that:

a. Over one-half (55.1%) called their programs "Outdoor Education." About one in ten (8.9%) used a combination of terms, such as "Outdoor and Environmental Education."
b. A majority of the respondents (63% of 694 districts, or 437) used some form of on-site resident experience either separately or in combination with other types of experiences. Use of resident sites varied with the grade level of the program and the percentage of elementary programs was higher (79%).

Statistically speaking, the State of California has been consistent in documenting the impact of resident outdoor education programs. Seven state-wide surveys were conducted between the 1953-54 school year and 1977-78. The following table illustrates the growth of these programs over a twenty-four year period:

	1953-54	1977-78	% Change
Number of Children	13,356	116,738	+744
Number of Schools	269	1,670	+520
Number of Districts	46	413	+798

The only national effort to collect attendance data was conducted by the Institute for Environmental, Camping, and Outdoor Education in 1978. This attempt was dependent on the ability of the various Depart-

Number of Children Attending Resident Outdoor School Programs, 1977-78

Alabama	NDS*	Kentucky	6,977	North Dakota	NDS
Alaska	NDS	Louisiana	NROEP	Ohio	38,556
Arizona	2,850	Maine	2,022	Oklahoma	730
Arkansas	NROEP**	Maryland	22,459	Oregon	20,000
California	116,738	Massachusetts	14,461	Pennsylvania	6,343
Colorado	30,913	Michigan	33,593	Rhode Island	143
Connecticut	280	Minnesota	35,700	South Carolina	NROEP
Delaware	72	Mississippi	NDS	South Dakota	900
District of Columbia	2,000	Missouri	16,283	Tennessee	1,900
Florida	2,224	Montana	100	Texas	7,126
Georgia	3,009	Nebraska	7,273	Utah	5,171
Hawaii	12,712	Nevada	NDS	Vermont	695
Idaho	1,107	New Hampshire	2,534	Virginia	NDS
Illinois	26,889	New Jersey	31,986	Washington	22,988
Indiana	5,900	New Mexico	NROEP	West Virginia	850
Iowa	3,847	New York	16,635	Wisconsin	14,033
Kansas	NDS	North Carolina	1,614	Wyoming	779
				National Total	521,171

*NDS = No Data Submitted

**NROEP = No Resident Outdoor Education Programs conducted in the State

ments of Education at the state level to aid the data collection process. Unfortunately, most states did not have this capability; consequently, the survey was pursued with the help of local organizations, associations, and resident centers. Recognizing the fact that the results listed in the table are not complete, they are presented in order to establish a bench mark for future surveys.

If any validity can be assigned to the above information, it appears that approximately 76% of the states (including the District of Columbia) have schools that provide resident outdoor education opportunities. It also appears that California is one state that has documented the impact of these programs within the various school districts. It is obvious that another attempt at a national survey is needed before a more definitive statement regarding the status of resident outdoor education programs in the United States can be made.

Selected References

1. Hammerman, Donald R., "An Historical Analysis of the Socio-Cultural Factors that Influenced the Development of Camping Education," Unpublished doctoral dissertation, Pennsylvania State University, 1961.
2. Melancon, Joseph C., Jr., "Status of Resident Outdoor School Programs in California, 1974-75," Unpublished master's thesis, San Francisco State University, 1976.
3. National Education Association, *Environmental Education in the Public Schools*. Washington, D.C.: Research Division, National Education Association, 1970.
4. Sharp, L. B. and Ernest G. Osborne, "Schools and Camping," *Progressive Education*. April, 1940.
5. St. Clair, Janet, "The Growth, Development and Present Status of School Camping in the United States," Unpublished paper, State University of Iowa, 1958.
6. St. Clair, Janet, "The Education Curriculum Philosophy of a Select Group of School Camps," Unpublished master's thesis, State University of Iowa, 1958.

EPILOGUE

On its "golden anniversary," resident outdoor education is accepted—conceptually and intellectually—as an integral part of the total school curriculum. Although few educators might doubt the values and benefits of such a learning experience, only a small percentage of children in America actually have the opportunity to attend a resident outdoor program during their school careers.

The various themes developed in the previous chapters have crystalized the essence of resident outdoor education as practiced in the United States from 1930-1980, and have highlighted the impact this curriculum innovation has had on American education. Outdoor education experienced steady growth throughout the 1940s and 1950s; and with the advent of the Elementary and Secondary Education Act of 1965, resident programs enjoyed a spectacular increase. The last decade has witnessed diversification of the basic philosophy and concepts of outdoor education so that there are now many forms and patterns for educators to choose from in addition to resident outdoor school programs.

During this period of time, American society has shifted from a population that was 44 percent rural and 56 percent urban in 1930 to a distribution pattern that is currently 73 percent metropolitan and 27 percent non-metropolitan. It is difficult to measure the impact upon countless numbers of children who, over the past fifty years, had their first experience to be absent from their primary community—their home and neighborhood—and placed in a new social structure. For some urban children, it might have been the first opportunity to experience the "natural" world rather extensively over a sustained period of time. Looking back, however, it can probably be claimed that:

a) School camping was an "alternative" to the "traditional" curriculum pattern long before the popularization of the term, "alternative education."

b) As a curriculum innovation, the resident outdoor education experience stressed "holism" along with teaching strategies that were compatible with this new teaching-learning environment; e.g., problem-solving; exploratory; self-discovery; and inquiry approaches to learning.

c) With "relationships" as the fourth "R" of the curriculum, these programs provided an opportunity for pupils to "see" their teachers as "human beings"; to enhance their own peer relationships; and to become better acquainted with their own "self-concepts."

d) In a country that is based upon democratic principles, the resident setting allowed for the establishment of a miniature community so that the pupils could experience democracy in action.

125

e) Before "ecology" became the slogan of the 1970s, many outdoor school programs provided students with their initial "awareness" experience with their environment and introduced them to principles and concepts of conservation and environmental education.

To ascertain the status of resident outdoor education with any degree of accuracy, on this fiftieth anniversary, is virtually impossible. Most states simply do not know the extent to which this program is being practiced. Just as past pioneers—like Vinal, Sharp, and Smith—provided leadership in their spheres of influence and displayed enthusiasm, idealism, and stamina; other individuals, acting alone and through organizations, are doing likewise today. Thus the traditions and beliefs of outdoor education continue to be perpetuated.

After five decades one might ask: Why haven't the schools done more to include a camping experience as an integral segment of the curriculum? Will educationists of the year 2000 A.D. look back upon the school people of 1938, as predicted by Schorling, or of 1980 and wonder—why? Will the future of school camping be similar to that projected for organized camping by James Mason—a decline in traditional camps?(2) Some parallel reasons might include the following:

a) a declining birth rate and decrease in the population of the school camp age constituency.

b) the increasing costs of resident outdoor school programs, which may not be matched by the public's perception of the program's effectiveness.

c) an increase in the variety of outdoor-related alternatives available for schools, e.g., day field trips, adventure bound, and environmental education.

d) the retirement from active educational roles of a generation of innovative and influential resident outdoor school leaders, who have been in leadership positions since the 1950s and 1960s.

Traditional school camping might decline for one or more of these reasons; but if the trend of the 1970s—The Period of New Directions—continues, the next period might well be labelled—"The Period of Experiential Education." A period in which the "form" or "structure" of the program (e.g., residential) is not the most important factor to be considered, but one in which the learning processes and teaching strategies are of greater significance. In pursuing this line of thinking, some outdoor educators believe that resident outdoor school practices will return to the essence of the outdoor education philosophy as stated by L. B. Sharp—"Those things which can best be taught in the outdoors should be taught there." George Donaldson, one of the "pioneers" in the outdoor education movement, has stated recently, "The great attraction which outdoor education held for many restive educators in its early day was its holistic, problem-centered style. Children and teachers went outdoors when the outdoors offered a better way of solving an educational problem or place to have wholesome, invigorating living experiences."(1)

Along with Donaldson, many of the outdoor leaders involved with the adventure/stress/challenge programs and outdoor living skills believe they have captured and returned to these philosophical fundamentals. "The new emphasis on open schools and schools without walls," according to Donaldson, "will reinforce the movement of outdoor education back to a balance among cognitive, affective, and psychomotor learning. Outdoor education will once again be education *in* the outdoors and *for* the outdoors."(1)

As American education enters the latter portion of the 20th century, there remain two major societal concerns—among many—that lend themselves to the principles and practices of outdoor education. One is mankind's age-old need to understand and to improve the quality of relationships with fellow humans (and with oneself); another is to understand and to improve the quality of one's relationships with the natural and physical environment. Studies have indicated that outdoor education programs possess the potential for making positive gains in relation to these two goals. Whether or not outdoor education programs are more effective in achieving these ends—from both a program quality and cost-effectiveness frame of reference—than any other curriculum practice has not been ascertained.

The preparation and development of teachers and leaders, at both the preservice and inservice levels, must continue to include outdoor living and learning experiences. In a society where one's life space, while growing up, is highly urbanized; educational institutions at all levels must guarantee that their charges will not become "culturally disadvantaged" because they lack outdoor experiences. In this era of life-long learning, educational opportunities in the outdoors must be extended to include the adult education sector as well as special populations.

Although leadership efforts on a regional and national basis have been exerted for over twenty-five years; there is not a strong national outdoor education sphere of influence that is operational. A few individual state associations and the Council for Outdoor Education appear to be the current "spark plugs" of the resident outdoor education movement. Just which organizational model will prove most beneficial and be most appropriate for this unique educational dimension is yet undetermined. A more effective means, however, must be created if outdoor education is to continue to influence educational programs in America.

Due to continually rising costs, some educators see resident outdoor schools in the future as a "luxury" item in the curriculum—available only to "well-to-do" communities and school districts. Many boards of education will ask, "Can we afford to do it, financially?"

The answer might best be stated with another question, "Can we afford not to do it, educationally?" Only the next fifty years will tell. The out-of-doors, as a laboratory for learning, is still needed for providing curriculum-related experiences that are holistic, humanistic, and compatible with principles of human growth and development.

Selected References

1. Donaldson, George W., and Donaldson, Alan D., "Outdoor Education: Its Promising Future," *Journal of Health, Physical Education, and Recreation,* April, 1972.
2. Mason, James A., "Uncertain Outposts: The Future of Camping and the Challenges of Its Past," An Occasional Paper Issued by the Fund for the Advancement of Camping, *Camping Magazine,* September-October, 1978.

Photography Credits

The photographs used in this commemorative book came from the following sources. Permission was granted for a one-time use, only. The copyrights for these pictures are retained by the various photographers. Questions or comments regarding the photographs should be directed to the appropriate source.

Burgess Publishing Company
7108 Ohms Lane
Minneapolis, MN 55435
(612) 831-1344

Permission granted to use pictures from *Teaching in the Outdoors*, 1964 & 1973.

William M. Hammerman
School of Education
San Francisco State University
1600 Holloway Avenue
San Francisco, CA 94132
(415) 469-1300

Photographs taken for the pilot resident outdoor education program for the Burris Laboratory School, Ball State Teachers College, Muncie, Indiana, 1958.

Northern Illinois University
Regional Services
DeKalb, IL 60115

Granted permission to use pictures taken at the Lorado Taft Field Campus, Oregon, Illinois, 1960s.

Phiz Mezey
Photographer
209 Upper Terrace
San Francisco, CA 94117
(415) 564-6685

Media specialist and photo essayist for the STEP Project, San Francisco State University, gave permission for use of pictures taken at Camp Leonard, 1966.

Gerald Morse
San Francisco YMCA Camp
Jones Gulch
La Honda, CA 94020
(415) 747-0221

Granted permission to use pictures taken at their Ropes Course.

Donald Rettew, Photographer
Box 261, Route 1
Robesonia, PA 19551
(215) 589-4225

A participant at National Camp and a member of the Outdoor Education Association. His photography represents the period of time, 1951-1961, when he worked with L. B. Sharp.